DAVID RUSSELL

SELF-PORTRAIT OF THE PAINTER

DAVID RUSSELL Self-Portrait of the Painter

DAVID RUSSELL © 2009 ISBN 978-1-4452-4950-6

FOREWORD

At the age of eighty-two, looking back, I can see how my life has developed with the usual regrets of lost opportunities, unfulfilled aspirations, mistakes of one sort or another. All the same I have had great moments of happiness and pleasure, and have been very fortunate: spoilt as a child and 'privileged' (as is now said) as an adult. Was that fortunate? Perhaps not, but it certainly gave me the chance as an artist to express myself without commercial pressures.

The great technological changes I have witnessed sometimes amaze me: the iPod, the computer on which I am writing this, the television which I first saw in 1937 as a small black-and-white shaky picture, and which is now in high definition on a quasi cinema screen. In the world of art I cannot really say there have been enormous changes: a painting is still colours on a canvas, the changes have been more in the acceptance of other media as 'fine art' (probably now an elitist expression.) I mean installations, video....non-touchable media.

I expect these notes will only interest people who know me, and that is more or less the audience these memoirs are aimed at. As well as being a record for myself of events that I may well otherwise forget in the future!

D.R. 2009
E & OE

1

ANTECEDENTS and CHILDHOOD

My father, David Russell, was born on 1st. May 1896 in Stenhousemuir, Falkirk, Scotland, the second son of Robert Mochrie and Agnes Hay Russell. He later took his mother's surname, having fallen out with his father. His elder brother George emigrated as a young man to Australia where he made good in the furniture business. David also left Scotland very young, and joined the army in the Great War, first in the Royal Horse Artillery, and then, after a hernia from riding, the Artists' Rifles at Osborne House in the Isle of Wight. The latter regiment suited him better, as at that time he had aspirations to be a singer (which did not come to fruition, as his voice did not have what it takes.) He made friends with some interesting writers and artists, for example Roy Horniman the author of 'Kind Hearts and Coronets.' He also talked of a conjurer called Collins who worked under the name of Co Ling Su.

It must have been about this time that my father met a man who was to be a great influence in his life: Sir Francis Hercy.

Sir Francis was last in line, with his sister and two brothers, of a family descending from Malveysin de Hercy, constable of Tykhill in 1221, and acquiring the estate of Grove, Nottingham.

Sir Francis remained a bachelor, as did his two brothers, and his sister Rowena died a spinster. Sir Francis had the nickname of 'The Hermit', I don't know why, and one of his brothers was 'The Bat', presumably because of his night-life. During the second world war the Bat is supposed to have said "I'd rather be bombed at the Berkeley than bored in Berkshire," (where the family seat was now, at Cruchfield in Winkfield, Berkshire.)

Sir Francis served at the War Ministry in recruitment during the Great War, and earned a CBE. He was also a Deputy Lieutenant of the City of London. It must have been in the army that he met my father, who after the war became his private secretary.

My father in his twenties

Sir Francis lived at 80 South Audley Street in Mayfair, where he had a chef and housekeeper, and entertained on quite a grand scale. He was an autocrat of the old school, a Catholic educated at Stonyhurst. He had been a great friend of George Harland Peck, who lived at 9 Belgrave Square, where he had an important collection of French paintings and furniture, including works by Chardin, Fragonard, Watteau and others. He owned the paint and varnish works of William Harland and Sons at Merton in Surrey, which was founded in 1796. The river Wandle ran through its grounds under a Chinoiserie wooden bridge, and the offices were housed in a splendid Georgian building..

George Harland Peck seems to have been a spendthrift, and when he died the place was in decline. To make matters worse his wife lost her mind, and her assets were administered by the Master in Lunacy. Sir Francis inherited much of their property, including the factory and the Belgrave Square house, but how this happened I do not know! The house suffered bomb damage in World War 2, as did the house in South Audley Street.

My father met my mother, Marjorie Elizabeth Cogle, at the Chelsea Arts ball in 1926. She was dressed as a Dresden shepherdess.

Marjorie's father, Henry George Cogle, was born in Plymouth in 1875. He started life as an engineer at the Devonport dockyard, but his life changed when studied art at the local art college. He was determined to become a painter, and after gaining the necessary diplomas he taught painting at Belfast Art School.

He married the daughter of a farmer from Chagford, Dartmoor, Sarah Frost, and my mother was born on 27th.March 1903. After Belfast the family moved to London, to Tite Street in Chelsea, and Henry taught at Battersea Polytechnic, where he later became head of department.

Marjorie grew up in this rather bohemian milieu, and studied music at the Guildhall School, piano and elocution. Her ambition was the stage, and this was soon realised when she auditioned for a part as a fairy in 'A Midsummer Night's Dream' at the Old Vic under Ben Greet. She met Lilian Bayliss and Sybil Thorndike with whom she developed a friendship and met up with later in life in North Wales.

Marjorie with her parents   Sir Francis in uniform

David and Marjorie were married at Marylebone Registry Office, and I was born the next year, on 15th June 1927, in Royal Avenue, Chelsea. We lived at 54 Chester Terrace in Belgravia, later to be renamed Chester Row. It was a small house with a basement and a garden. We had a cook and I had a nanny, and later a French governess. I had my own room, but sometimes felt lonely in my cot and got into bed with my parents. In the year of the general strike my father drove a bus. We had a canary, a gramophone, and the wireless. The songs I remember in my early years were 'Tiptoe through the Tulips', 'The Peanut Vendor', and 'Ours is a nice house, ours is!'

Marjorie gave up her career to become a wife and mother, perhaps also because in those days it was less than respectable to be an actress. But she kept many of her old friends from the theatre: Jessie Matthews, Beatrice Lillie, Frankie Lawton (whom she almost married,) and Evelyn Laye.

I remember the street criers, looking out of the living room window: they must have been near their end. The muffin man, with a bell and tray on his head, the costermonger, the woman with a basket crying 'Buy my sweet lavender!' Also the lamplighters with their long poles, lighting the gaslamps. Sometimes on Sundays we would go shopping at the Houndsditch Warehouse, in a Jewish quarter of London, the only place open on Sundays.

I remember the cook showing me how to make a jam tart, and this remained in my bedroom for some weeks with its plaited pastry strips on top. I had a red Indian outfit with headdress and tomahawk, and a sailor suit.

Sir Francis had bought a maisonette in Brighton, at no. 6 Lewes Crescent, and we often went there for holidays in his Rolls Royce complete with cat, canary, cook and chauffeur. As a small child I remember spending happy Christmases there with a big tree, and presents numbered for the recipients....spoilt child that I was, I was always number one!

In Lewes Crescent there was a big garden with a key for residents. There was a 'horseshoe' of flints as a shelter from the wind, and a mysterious tunnel that went under the road to another garden on the seafront which was full of butterflies.

The head gardener was named Holinshed, like the chronicler, and he said one day to Sir Francis "Did you ever 'ear tell of 'Arrison Ainsworth? Well, he wrote a book about Ovingdean Grange, and I come from Ovingdean!" (A village on the South Downs.)

Back in London I started school at Gibbs's from about the age of four. It was in Sloane Street, the Sloane Square end, opposite Holy Trinity church. At the back it gave onto Pavilion Road, and there was a playground and carpenter's shop.

Gibbs's was a delightful school, with interesting boys whose parents mostly lived in Chelsea. We had a French Mademoiselle, Mlle Chaussat, who taught with large oilskin posters of the farmyard, or the salon, and we had to learn the names of the animals, or the furniture. There were also drawing and music lessons, and a boy scout or rather Wolf Cub group. We had a talk by the famous phoney 'Grey Owl' American Indian.

Peter Ustinov had just left when I arrived there, but they still talked about 'Usty-Wusty'. Other interesting boys included the son of David Devant the magician, and of course the boys all wanted to know the secrets of his tricks. There was also Robert Kennedy for a while, and my future landlord in Florence, Neri Capponi. The only thing I hated was the football every week at Harrods grounds in Barnes. There I agree entirely with Sir Michel Howard in his autobiography.

It was not far to walk to school from Chester Terrace, but when I was about six, we moved to 93 Sloane Street, near the Cadogan Hotel. The day we moved we had lunch at the Royal Court hotel, and saw our removals van making its way around Sloane Square.

Marjorie with me in Brighton

The new flat was very exciting: it was built around the lift and occupied the whole of the fifth floor. There was a maid's room and a dressing-room for my father. The actor Rex Harrison lived on the floor above, and my mother told me she heard him rowing all the time with Lily Palmer.

We had the key of Cadogan Gardens opposite, and that was great for playing with schoolfriends. Also at the top of Sloane Street there were two important tea-shops, Searcy and Tansley on the left, and Fullers opposite. My mother was friendly with one of the Searcy brothers, and we always got a good table for lunch or tea. My favourites at Fullers were the chocolate boxes, and the coffee cake with walnuts.

Sloane Street was not as chic as it is today. Towards the bottom of the street was the Golden Bud restaurant, a simple but good place. Around the corner was the Christian Science church, with a kind of minaret that I could see from my bedroom window, and imagine that there was a Rapunzel princess on the balcony.

My parents bought new furniture for the flat from Mrs Shields, an art deco designer of the day, and I had a present of a Challen baby grand piano on which I had lessons from Miss Vivash, a forbidding teacher from whom I used to hide under the piano. We also had a Czech maid, Tilda, who lived in and made enormous strudels while chain-smoking and reading detective novels in English.

But before Tilda there was another maid, and with her I had a serious accident. One evening when my parents were out I chased her around the flat, when she shut the glass door of the kitchen. I banged on it and cut my left wrist. The poor girl was frantic: she bandaged my wrist and took me down Sloane Street to Allsop and Quiller, the chemists, leaving a trail of blood down the street. The chemist put a tourniquet on my arm, and very luckily the cut just missed the artery, but cut the tendon of my fourth finger. I was very proud of the fourteen stitches I had in hospital. The poor maid was sacked. I was sorry as I liked her.

Every Sunday we would go and have tea with Sir Francis in South Audley Street. He would invariably have a chocolate cake from Gunters around the corner, with rolls of chocolate on top. At Christmas he would have a huge cracker with presents inside, and one Christmas he gave me a copy of the Children's Encyclopaedia which I have to this day.

A typical Edwardian, he liked to read sentimental poems aloud, and I remember one of a little girl dying on a bed of roses, and it had the tears streaming down his face.

I suppose I was like a surrogate child to my Godfather, and he wrote

Family at Chester Terrace in the garden

angry letters to my parents when they went off to the South of France leaving me in the care of a very strict and unpleasant nanny.

Back in London I drew and painted a lot, encouraged by my mother and grandfather who had come to live not far away in Ebury Street. At school Miss Baynes taught art. I did a portrait of her, and we had to draw a still-life from memory, as well as invented subjects. I liked 'making things' often out of cardboard boxes. I made the Crown Jewels in paper, and a scrolling Rupert the Bear from a shoebox, using cutouts from the Daily Express.

There was also the cinema and wireless. I saw Greta Garbo in Anna Karenina at what is now the Royal Court theatre, and Public Enemy Number One at the Classic, on the corner of Markham Street. The owner, Basil Clavering, was a friend of my parents and so we always had free seats in the circle.

One day day Sir Francis took me in the Rolls to the West End to look at antique shops. He found two statuettes of Voltaire and Rousseau in Bond Street, which doubtless had belonged to the Harland Pecks. He said I had brought him luck. I still have the statuettes.

I made some good friends at Gibbs's, one of whom was Oliver Evans Palmer, and his parents became friends with mine. Oliver's father was an architect, and they lived nearby in a modern house in Elystan Place. Chelsea in those days was like a village, it had its big stores like Sainsbury and Woolworth, but also bakeries with old-fashioned cottage loaves, and fishmongers and greengrocers.

Oliver (left) & David (right) at Gibbs's

My grandfather had retired from Battersea Polytechnic while I was at Gibbs's school and was able to concentrate on his own work, as well as teaching me a lot. He and my grandmother had a house in South Devon, at Newton Ferrers, on the river Yealm. My mother and I often went down to Devon for holidays, and would drive in Harry's, (my grandfather's) Austin into Plymouth, and have tea at Goodbody's tea-room which boasted a ladies' string quartet. And then days by the sea, or on Dartmoor. Harry had an etching press at Waydown, their house, and he showed me how to print. There was also an apple orchard; he sold the fruit for cider every year. My grandmother was a very experienced embroideress and had made clothes for the dioramas at the Commonwealth Exhibition in the nineteen-twenties. On one holiday I was on my own with my grandparents, as my parents had gone to visit friends in Sweden, and I had refused to go. I had a tent in the garden where I slept, and in the evenings we would make a camp fire and sing songs. I read a great deal, and I remember once my grandmother bought me a book, and told me 'that must last a week!'

We also went to Scotland for holidays on the night-train, waking up in Edinburgh and having breakfast at the Great Eastern Hotel, pancakes and porridge. In 1936 we had a big family reunion, when my paternal grandmother was still alive, in Perth where she lived. In the photograph on the next page I am second from left in the front row, my cousin Agnes next to me, then my uncle George, my grandmother and my father. My mother is second from right in the back row. I remember on this same visit staying at Gleneagles Hotel, and taking a horse-drawn bus to Lake Katrine. I was allowed to sit with the coachman. It was so cold I saw icicles dangling from his nose.

We also went to Aviemore and the Cairngorms, and Loch Awe taking the car on the train from London.

Nearby was the mountain Ben Cruachan, which was for sale with a golf course and a house. The sale was for the entire mountain!

David (left) and Oliver today

Family reunion in Perth, 1936

My father thought seriously about buying the property, but it would have needed a lot of courage and we were a long way away from Scotland. But it was only £6000!

When I was about eight years old I was sent to boarding school. This was to Ludgrove, one of the preparatory schools for Eton, and which was located at Barnet, north London.

This was very daunting for me, as apart from holidays with my grandparents, and the odd scout jamboree, I had never slept away from home. But there were one or two friends from Gibbs's, and I settled in.

There was considerable emphasis on sports, and I hated both football and cricket, however there were also fives courts, and I liked the geometry of this game. There were some interesting boys at Ludgrove, for example Guerlain of the perfume dynasty, Pulman of the trains, the Worsley brothers whose sister married the Duke of Kent, Pilkington of the glass.

I started in April 1937, and we were given special leave for the coronation of George VI: unfortunately I was ill in hospital for the event, but listened on the wireless. But before that, with my parents and Sir Francis, we went to the funeral of George V as Sir Francis knew one of the keepers in Hyde Park, and we had a fine view from his lodge on a rainy day in Park Lane. I should mention also that Sir Francis had a key to Hamilton Gardens in Park Lane, and as a small boy I often played there, and at least once played ring-a-ring-a-roses with princesses Elizabeth and Margaret Rose who lived nearby, our nannies chatting on a bench.

Later the same year Ludgrove moved to Wixenford, near Wokingham in Berkshire, being a big estate with private chapel, golf course and sports fields. Miss Lemon was the matron who looked after our health, and there was another nurse with whom another boy, Aspinall, and I had an assignation in the lavatory at night to ask about eggs, that is human eggs - a subject about which we knew little!

Robin Milford was our distinguished music teacher, and I continued my piano efforts, Mr. Bowmar-Porter taught a very old-fashioned form of drawing of which I do not think my grandfather would greatly have approved , as he was now in love with the Impressionists.

The Headmaster of Ludgrove was A.T.Barber, with T.W.Shaw. I have to say I did not take to Mr. Barber at all. He was very sadistic, and one of his punishments for these small boys was marching around the gymnasium for an hour or so holding a rifle above their heads. With some other boys we decided to steal his 'drill book', which listed all the punishments he had given, especially to the boys with a title of whom there were quite a few.

We hid the book in the carpentry shop for a while, and when it was discovered to be missing all the boys were called into a classroom and asked to own up, otherwise privileges were to be withdrawn.

Our next move was to throw the book into the middle of the school pond. I cannot remember if we owned up to this dastardly act, or if Barber found out another way, but he took me to the side of the pond and said "Would you treat a valuable book of your father's like this?" I replied that my father didn't have disgusting books like that, which of course infuriated him. I do not remember how many strokes of the cane I received, but I remember noting that Barber was frothing at the mouth as he caned me.

I had one other contretemps: my friend John Aspinall was ill in the school sanatorium, and I had sent away for some girlie magazines, nothing very obscene these days, but then outrageously illicit. I sent them, via the headmaster's wife up to the sanatorium rolled up in a copy of Country Life. I should have chosen another magazine, for she opened it and discovered the incriminating document. I was caned for that too, but fortunately I was nearing the end of my time at Ludgrove, and my father took me away in the summer of 1939.

I had good reports at Ludgrove, and liked some of the masters, particularly Mr.Head the maths master for whom I did a drawing before I left, (he asked me if I liked Dalì, but pronouncing his name as Daily so that I did not know whom he was talking about,) and also Mr.Beale who taught me a way of tying my shoelaces, but who later committed suicide.

But I was happy to see the back of this school: the emphasis on sporting achievements I found especially difficult.

Early photo of mother, Sir Francis, & father

In the summer of 1939 my father gave up the flat in Sloane Street: it was getting too expensive at £500 a year. We left for Torquay with Sir Francis, where my grandparents were now staying, renting a flat near the harbour. We stayed some time at the Imperial Hotel, and then Sir Francis decided to rent a big manor house in Surrey, Frensham Beale Manor.

This was a delightful stone house with a private chapel, swimming-pool, squash court, and a brook running into Frensham Ponds.

It was here in September we heard the declaration of war on the wireless. We had settled in with two dogs, a black cocker called Jill, and a scotty, and friends came to stay to play squash and dive into the pool.

However this soon changed. Lord Alexander, commander of the 1st. infantry division, arrived to post his troops in our squash court, Gordon Highlanders. A searchlight was set up in the field above the house, and a soldier stationed outside my father's bedroom, and if the telephone rang during the night my father was to leap out of bed and tell the soldier to run up the hill and turn on the searchlight! The troops were also very happy to use the splendid pool, and life became quite difficult for us.

Then Sir Francis had a bright idea. His best friend was Lord Granville, who was married to Rosie, the Queen Mother's sister. He was a bluff sailor, nicknamed 'Wisp'. His family had a house at the village of Holmbury St. Mary in Surrey, and he had to leave it as he was appointed to the Governorship of the Isle of Man. Would it be possible to rent it, or would it be requisitioned in the same way as Frensham Beale Manor?

In the event Wisp was happy to rent the house for the duration of the war, as it was unlikely to be requisitioned , and he could leave his servants in situ. We moved there in 1940, Sir Francis moving his furniture from his London house, as being less likely to be bombed.

I remember one of Wisp's footmen in uniform with breeches and frogging, and there were two gardeners and a boy. Sir Francis brought his own cook, Mrs. McVeigh, his chauffeur Foster, and butler Choak. We all took to the house immediately with its beautiful gardens and views.

Radnor House, Holmbury St.Mary, Surrey

Radnor became very important in my life. It had a marvellous atmosphere and charm. It was originally a thirteenth century house on the slopes of Holmbury Hill in Surrey, facing south towards the coast. In fact on a clear day you could see the sea through the 'Shoreham Gap'.

It had been improved by Norman Shaw, and only the kitchen with its huge stone slab floor was probably original. Countess Castalia Granville in the mid-nineteenth century had a great interest in gardening and had planted a great many trees and shrubs, in fact her copy of Robinson's 'The English Flower Garden' enabled me to identify many of the subjects in the garden, as she had ticked them in the book.

But this was later. For the present Earl Granville's furniture remained in the house, and his gardener in the garden, looking after the peaches and melons in the greenhouse. There was a superb Chinese cabinet which I wrote a poem about, with mysterious hidden drawers. There was a set of the Dictionary of National Biography, and then there was Sir Francis's Ruff's Guide to the Turf in several dozen volumes. We had my Challen piano from London, and the eighteenth-century Italian walnut credenza which had been in the hall of the Sloane Street flat, and was a present from my father to my mother.

There was also the Stock family. Old Stock had been a groom to Nina Granville, Wisp's mother, and he and his wife and daughter lived in a part of the house which I never saw until much later. Lady Granville, apart from having the village renamed from Felday to Holmbury St.Mary, as rumour had it, kept her horses in the stables near the house, and drove down from London, where she had a grace-and-favour apartment in Kensington Palace, with a coach and pair.

Many years later I was alone in the house, and a man rang the bell. He told me that many years ago, at the beginning of the twentieth century, he had been a footman for Lady Granville, and he had recently come back to England from Canada where he had lived for many years. He was curious to revisit the house, and told me that when he was working at Radnor he had seen Halley's Comet, which must have been 1910.

He had many anecdotes about Lady Granville, who seems to have been a martinet, and had sacked a maidservant for picking violets from the long border in front of the house. I showed him the servants' hall, which was now unused. He talked about Christmas festivities for the servants, and said it was one of the happiest times of his life.

More about Radnor later, after the war..

Marjorie with her Pekinese, Chang, won in a raffle

Marjorie in a field   Henry Cogle: Marjorie as a fairy. Oil on canvas

Henry Cogle: Portrait of Marjorie in red beret   Henry Cogle: Portait of Marjorie in blue hat

Albert Moody: Henry Cogle. Oil on canvas

Grandfather at the easel

Henry Cogle: Self-portrait, etching

Grandfather in his fifties

2

THE WAR and ETON

I cannot remember how long we stayed at Radnor, but the war began to be heard overhead, and German incendiary bombs dropped nearby in the fields. We started to sleep on camp beds in the ground-floor corridor: the house had only two floors, except for a loft bedroom, but was long, a wing having been added in 1904. There were about 25 rooms.

There was also a cellar, but that was cold and dank, and I do not remember ever sleeping there. Choak the butler had left us later to become a hairdresser in Guildford, and Foster the chauffeur was to join the Royal Air Force as Wing Commander.

Sir Francis had a friend in North Wales, Clough Williams-Ellis, who had transformed a headland near Portmadoc (as it then was,) into a hotel village: Portmeirion. Sir Francis decided to drive up there in his Rolls with Foster, rent a suite in the main hotel, and we would join him later if all went well. My godfather was then in his sixties, and not in very good health. At some point on the journey he had to leave the car to shelter in a ditch as bombs were falling around.

My father also had a Rolls-Royce, a more trendy model with grey leather seats, and after a week or two we drove up to join Sir Francis, leaving Mrs. McVeigh as well as Tilda at Radnor. I was very sad to leave, but curious to see Wales and this strange hotel. My parents were now worried about my education, having said goodbye to Ludgrove.

The hotel was extraordinary, later featured in a TV drama, 'The Prisoner' which I never saw. But during the war it was a refuge for exiles, for example King Zog of Albania with his bodyguards, Cicely Courtnedge and Jack Hulbert, and Noel Coward who wrote 'Blithe Spirit' while we were there, and sang in the bar in the evenings.

The manager was Jim Wylie, who later went to live in Tangier, and Clough himself turned up occasionally in his yellow stockings. The atmosphere was quite informal. We ate in the restaurant most evenings and I remember the menu becoming very monotonous: Garbure Soup featuring frequently. However the restaurant manager was a trained make-up artist and gave a show in the Portmadoc Theatre inviting the audience on to the stage to be made up as various characters.

There was also an American, Mrs. Cornelius who spent long hours gambling at backgammon, and an Australian woman, Rita Kerr, who became a great friend of my mother, and who, for some reason, was thrown out of the hotel by Jim Wylie, and rented a house near Penrhyndaedraeth.

Another friend of my mother at the hotel was Sue Kellino, who had divorced from Roy Kellino the cameraman, who later became a director. She asked me why my mother had never been divorced, and I was quite shocked!

My parents were worried about my education as I was now 13, and they looked for a school for me in the neighbourhood, including Daedraeth Castle, then a school. Instead Sir Francis found me a tutor, Harry Kent, who lived in the hotel. He taught me the usual subjects, but was dry as dust, and I wrote scurrilous poems about him. I suppose I was in a difficult position: an only child having hated my last school, Ludgrove, and now a kind of war exile in an adults' world. However there were compensations. On the headland behind the hotel was an enormous garden created by George Haigh who had a nearby house. This was an exciting place for walks: there were caves, a temple, a waterfall, and rhododendron overgrown alleyways. Haigh had planted magnificent specimens of magnolias and other trees, and I got to know the shortcuts to the sea, and the ways around the gardens of I do not know how many acres. I had a collie called Rex who followed me around.

As I said, there were few children there, but one day a film team arrived to make a Will Hay film in the estuary. It may have been 'The Ghost of St.Michael's', but I am not sure. Anyhow there were two child actors, a boy and a girl, and I fell for the girl as we played at climbing ropes in the top floor gymnasium!

I also experienced my first 'wet dreams' in my bedroom. I was startled at this physical manifestation, my parents never having talked to me about sex. I kept it to myself.

The next move was to a house across the estuary which Sir Francis had spotted, and I suppose being fed up with this hotel life, albeit with excursions to Portmadoc and Bettws-y- Coed it was time for a change.

The house, Maes-y-Neuadd, or the house in a field, belonged to Colonel Kirkby, a Yorkshireman. It was a big stone house with out-buildings, and 10,000 acres of land, comprising trout lakes and hillside. Sir Francis rented the house 'for the duration', my father going down to Radnor from time to time to keep an eye on things both at Radnor, and William Harland and Son.

There was a laundry, garages, kennels, dairy, and a stream passing by, strong enough to power a generator, as there was no mains current. There was a huge walled kitchen garden looked after by Williams, the gardener, and a big kitchen with an Aga.

Tilda came up from Radnor and took charge of the kitchen, with the help of Blodwen a local girl, and Rosa a sixteen year old with red hair. There was a big sitting-room on the ground floor, a dining-room, and upstairs a bat-haunted billiards room. Kirkby had left his furniture, and in a games room I found some of his daughters' books: old copies of the Strand Magazine with the original Sherlock Holmes stories, and a fan magazine about Clark Gable. For reading matter I subscribed to the Classics Book Club which sent books by post. as did the London Library.

David and grandparents at Maes-y-Neuadd

I had a bicycle for a birthday present: I had never ridden one before, except for my tricycle in Brighton, but the house being on a hillside it was not very practical. I relied on my father to drive into Harlech, not far away, to go to the shops and the cinema on a Saturday. A cinema that was most uncomfortable, the seats being hard wooden benches.

Near us lived Richard Hughes, the author of 'High Wind in Jamaica,' but I don't recall ever meeting him, and Lord Harlech who had a big estate lower down the hill. Also on the way to Harlech lived the German mother of Robert and Charles Graves. It seems Charles had stayed at Maes-y-Neuadd and had seen the ghost of a white dog which was supposed to haunt the house.

My parents looked in vain for a suitable school for me. I was still down for Eton, but had to get up to scratch in Classics and Maths. Eventually a tutor came to stay: Mr. Townsend. He was much more agreeable than Harry Kent, and gave me lessons in the billiard room. He was a great cyclist, and bicycled all the way from London where he had a flat. He was also tutoring two other boys for Eton, Grosvenor and Fairbairn.

In spite of the rationing we did rather well as Jim Wylie used to drive over from Portmeirion and bring us salmon and young lamb, and there were trout in the various lakes on the property.

I suppose my family's slight feeling of guilt at escaping the rigours of war was assuaged by the idea that Sir Francis was too infirm to suffer the bombs down at Radnor. It was true that he had heart problems, and had to sit down on the landing half-way up the staircase, and he now always walked with a stick. He was still meticulous about dressing, although the spats of the old days were now gone. However he was not very happy about the lack of interesting social life at Talsarnau, our village.

Every month or so Jack Benson, the secretary of William Harland and Son would come up to Wales by train and go through the accounts. My godfather was very punctilious about keeping documents. Not long ago I found all the letters about my education, from Gibbs's to Oxford carefully preserved in manila envelopes. Also all my letters to him, the Christmas cards which I have always made, and other drawings. It is true he was like a grandfather to me, but perhaps I did not appreciate his kindness at the time.

Instead I was closer to my own grandfather, the painter. My mother also painted, and so I felt more attraction to that side of my family. Sir Francis was an extraordinary relic of a bygone age in many ways: scrupulous about manners and social niceties, a snob, an eccentric: for example he had a whole cast of characters he had known, like Velvet O'Beale who could do no two things equal, Mrs. Muspratti who would push her plate away exclaming "Too rich!" He took to thinking he was no longer appreciated, and said 'I am just a BODOTC,' a bit of dirt on the carpet. On the other hand he had a great knowledge of literature, he could recite the whole of Hamlet, quite an achievement, and one of his ancestors was Richard Lovelace the poet. Although I have sold his Louis Vuitton trunks, I still have his bamboo shooting stick. By all accounts he was a very good shot in his youth, and won prizes in clay pigeon shooting at Montecarlo.

Sir Francis's family had sent their children to Eton in the sixteenth century, and he was very keen for me to be educated there. My father, on his suggestion, had tried to put me down as far back as 1928,and had now found a place in J.M.Peterson's house in autumn 1941, after a lot of correspondence. Here is a letter he wrote to me after I had started at Eton:

My Dear "Uz"

First I must congratulate you most heartily on getting to Eton a year after time. I hope you will thank God that your father and mother worked this for you and asked Him to make you a success.

I feel sure you will be all right and good and that you will make up your mind to work very hard this first term so as to keep your place.

Be sure to thank Mr. Peterson for taking you into his house when you meet him at lunch before the 17th. and remember it is best never to have any question with, or contradict any master, always assume they are right even if you doubt it.

Above all never forget your prayers night and morning and then I know you will be happy and good and will get on with everyone.

It is very dull here without you and I am sure Judy misses you still, tho' Peter seems quite to have taken to Tilda. Be sure neither miss you as much as I do!

This is the last time I shall write to "Master David" it must be "Esquire" in future.

All my love to you dear child and be sure I shall be thinking of you every day. God bless you!

Your devoted old
Goffie

Judy that he refers to was our golden cocker spaniel, and Peter a chinchilla cat. And my nickname, in the family only, was 'Uz' or 'Uzzy', I don't know why.

It can be seen from this letter, and others, the immense affection 'Goffie' had for me. I found his advice quite difficult to live up to. He was from a very different generation, and to some extent I resented his subsuming my father's authority.

But I suppose my father accepted the fact that Sir Francis knew best and had my interests at heart. As I said before, I was more torn between my father and Sir Francis on the one hand, and my mother and her father on the other, who represented something very different: the world of art and freedom, and a different social background.

Around this time my grandparents came up to North Wales, never liking to be away from their only daughter for long, and they decided to settle in Wales for the war.

Sir Francis aged 64

and they rented a flat at Penrhyndaedraeth on the other side of the estuary.

My grandfather became very fond of his Welsh neighbours, going to the pub and perhaps recalling his days in Ireland. He began painting landscapes, the lakes nearby like Trawsfynydd.

So the time came when I started at Eton. Peterson's house, Carter house, was opposite the school yard and the chapel. A condemned building, which however was still being used. A sort of rabbit-warren of boys' rooms, as unlike the dormitories at Ludgrove, every boy had a room to himself, with a 'burry' or bureau, a bed that let down from the wall, and table and chairs.

my grandfather at his easel

There was an initiation ceremony mainly consisting of questions about the colours of the various houses, but nothing too exhorbitant. The new boys had to get together in 'messes', or small groups of three or four, to eat or study in the evenings. My group was James Coats, Martin Evans, and Adrian House and Michael Straker.

Morning school was at 7.30, and we learnt the technique of dressing very quickly, rushing downstairs and grabbing some fruit by the doorway, and arriving in the classroom. If we were there before the beak, or master, we could do a 'run' back home, stopping at the Bursar's office on the way to report what had happened. This involved knowing your way about to avoid meeting the beak on the way.

Then there was breakfast, and chapel. Lower chapel for the younger boys. I soon became drawn into the lower chapel choir (the College Chapel having a 'professional' choir) and had the task of leading the choristers into their pews on the two sides of the aisle, holding a large cross.

I enjoyed this: the music and the ritual, the choir practice once a week. The Precentor at Eton at the time was Doctor Henry Lee, a small Devonian whose feet barely reached the organ pedals, but a great musician. I was only sacked from these duties when I began to grow a moustache!

Dr. Coneybeare was in charge of us choristers, his name being quite appropriate: a big man with a big hug for his favourites!

My housemaster was J.M.Peterson, a God-fearing classicist, with a reddish countenance. He was married with two children, but his wife sadly died while I was at Carter House. He was a great Eton Fives player, and later became headmaster of Shrewsbury, his old school

In his letters to my father Peterson talks of my artistic talents, of my untidiness (sticking too many things on the walls of my room) but praising my helping the house by taking up the 'cello in the school orchestra.

In fact one of the reasons I took up the 'cello was to strengthen the fourth finger of my left hand, of which the tendon was weak, due to the accident I mentioned before. But I enjoyed the instrument, except for taking it on the train to North Wales in the holidays.

I forget the name of the 'cello teacher, but Dr Dunhill, a very well respected musician and composer, was in charge at the Music Schools. I remember with great pleasure playing Mozart's piano Quartet no. 1, with Nicholas Mosley piano, and Jeremy Thorpe violin. Simon Streatfeild viola.I have loved this piano quartet ever since. Streatfeild went on to become a professional musician, and Thorpe leader of the Liberal party.

Every day we had to do a 'time'. This consisted of exercise of one sort or another.In the winter it could be a run, and in the summer you were a 'dry bob' (cricket) or 'wet bob' (rowing on the Thames.)

We ticked our names off on a list in the hallway of the house. I often went for a walk (which I think was allowed) with David Lutyens, a boy from another house, and the least athletic person one could imagine. We talked about literature and art. But one day I was in fact practising the 'cello at the Music Schools, and somebody saw me and I was denounced and beaten. It was usually nine strokes with trousers down, in the 'Library', which was a sort of prefects' clubroom.

In those days fagging was still the practice: the older boys had younger boys as servants. I had the bad luck to be the fag of a boy called Wheatley who was the son of the head of the London Police. I had to make toast for him with a toasting fork over a coal fire which I also had to keep blazing. For some reason one day I was lax in my duties, and beaten severely. I think Wheatley was later expelled for drunkenness.

I later had two fags of my own, Guinness and Kirwan-Taylor, but I let them off most of the time, remembering my own humiliating experiences with Wheatley.

The other tiresome practice was 'Calling Boy' outside the Library. The younger boys had to come running, and the last to arrived usually had to take a message to another house. My room was in the depths of Carter house, so I was always the last to arrive. There were dire consequences if you did not obey the call, and once I was drawing an elaborate map with a fine mapping pen, and of course the ink splattered everywhere as I jumped up. In the evening we cooked in our rooms. My father sent chickens by post from Wales, which usually ended up crawling with maggots. There was a Fullers in Windsor, and I used my coupons to buy coffee cakes.

Of course the Drawing Schools were a great attraction for me. The art master was Wilfred Blunt, whose brother Anthony was later to become notorious as a spy for the Russians, but who was also a great expert on Poussin.

There was also a pottery class under LLewelyn Menzies-Jones, a rather austere and eccentric Welshman.

Blunt was also a baritone, and in school concerts would let fly with the Barber of Seville aria. He had also done a rather fine copy of an El Greco.

The Drawing Schools were a sort of haven for me, on the way from Jack's sock shop (otherwise tuck shop,) and the fives courts. Peterson was a great fives player, and following on from Ludgrove, this was really the only game I enjoyed. I briefly became a wet-bob, but my whiff (skiff) sank on two occasions in the Thames, and of course I got into trouble.

This is a report from Wilfred Blunt:

The Drawing Schools
Michaelmas 1940

<u>D Russell</u>

I was frankly staggered by the work which he brought back after the holidays. Both for quantity and quality it surpassed anything to which we are accustomed. Any criticism of his abstract paintings is immediately silenced by the evidence of the remainder that he can draw really well, in a straightforward way, when he chooses to do so. Painters and critics with views as widely apart as Sir Kenneth Clarke and Mr Oswald Birley have been unwaveringly impressed with his work, and I feel certain that great success lies ahead..

WWB

M'Tutor Jack Peterson with house cups

Although I do not recall seeing many important exhibitions in London during the war years, there were the National Gallery concerts with Dame Myra Hess, and I was able to go to London on my way up to North Wales, staying at the Connaught Hotel. Also from Mount Street Sir Francis ordered grouse and pheasants to be sent to Carter House for the boys, who were not too happy that he had not shot them himself!

I did a lot of drawing and painting at the Drawing Schools, but also became interested in mathematics, and took this as my subject when it became necessary to 'specialise.' I also visited the school library a lot, and played chess with Peter Swinnerton-Dyer, at 16 a brilliant mathematician who was unteachable at Eton, and called on by the War Office to make calculations. He told me his future was more or less ordained in advance, and in fact he became vice-chancellor of Cambridge University.

In the absence of any female companionship of our own age at Eton, apart from M'Dame (the house matron and something more,) and the boys' maids, there were sentimental attachments between older and younger boys. In a strange way, although not much sexuality was involved, this presented a microcosm of the great world of Society outside. There was also a lot of snobbery and anti-semitism, and I think a German boy in our house suffered some abuse.

Peterson had to look after the son of Anthony Eden who later became Prime Minister, and the son of William Collins, the publisher of the bible, as well as John Astor, Corbett Woodall who became a television newsreader. and Edward Fitzroy, the son of the Duke of Grafton.

From time to time Peterson would knock on our doors in the evening, when we were in bed, and give us a homily about sex and its perils. This was

Dr.Coneybeare, Eton Lower Master

Carter House

usually a rather embarrassing affair, some injunctions about self-abuse, the dangerous side of women in general, bathed in a religious light. I have to say my father did not do much better, and all I learned about sex was from a doctor's son at Gibbs's and a rather badly informed boy at Ludgrove. I was shy about asking.

One of the senior boys in our house was Brandon Rhys-Williams, very well-read and urbane, who introduced me to the writings of Freud and Jung. I think his grandmother was Ouida, or another exotic Victorian novelist. But he seemed more sophisticated than most of the others. He later became MP for Kensington.

I got into trouble pinning too many drawings on my walls, as well as dropping an erotic drawing out of the window which was found by the porter, luckily, who brought it back to me.

On the whole my reports were good, though I was considered shy and not very outgoing. I did well in Greek verses, and mathematics. But I hated the Field Game, which was an Eton hybrid of football and rugby.

I ended up able to play tennis, my last halves.

JMP's moved from Carter House to a much more recent house overlooking the playing fields. As time went on I was elected to 'Debate', which was a sort of preparation for 'The Library.' There were some actual debates, and a leaving ceremony which I refused to attend, before leaving Eton. I was considered Bolshy, which meant resisting the rules, and it was true. Nowadays rules have become 'Guidelines', but meaning exactly the same, but trying to give the impression that you are at liberty to disobey. (Human Rights!)

In June 1944 the flying bombs from Germany started to appear over Eton. You heard a buzzing, and when it stopped you knew the bomb had fallen. Claudius Elliott, the Headmaster sent a letter to all parents asking whether they would like their boys to sleep in the shelter nearby, or stay in their rooms. I remember staying at least a couple of nights down there, it was quite an adventure, but in fact I don't think there was a great deal of damage.

In letters to my parents in North Wales, I see that at one time I exhibited 14 paintings at the drawing schools,and wrote an essay on the respective merits of Dali and Picasso. I won the Gunther prize for art, and did my first self-portrait. The painter Kathleen Mann bought two of my paintings, the first sales I had made.

drawing done at Eton

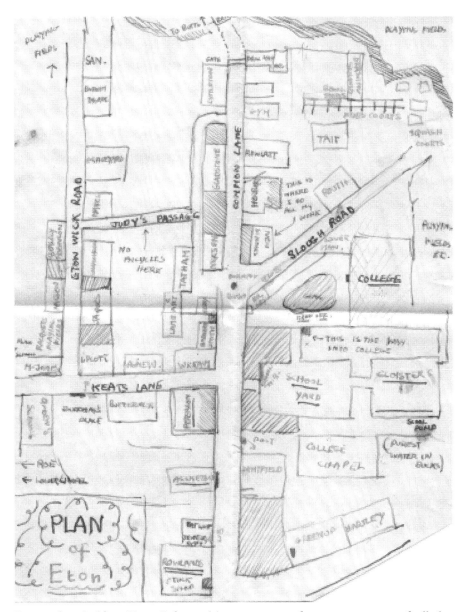

In my first half at Eton I drew this map to send to my parents, of all the houses in Eton and where they were placed. Carter House can be seen in the centre, just below the 'Burning Bush.'

Not far away was the school library where I spent a lot of time, in fact I wrote a sonnet about it which was published in the Eton Chronicle. Also nearby in the New Schools I worked on a mural under Blunt's direction, I think with a Homeric theme. At least I remember painting a Greek soldier with a shield in a battle scene.

The war meant a shortage of food, and although there were also coupons for clothes, that does not seem to have affected our uniforms of tails and top-hat. The tails had big pockets for books!

I enjoyed morning service in College Chapel. As well as being a beautiful building, the quiet and the ritual pleased me. Having been baptised at the Church of Scotland in Pont Street, I was now confirmed by the Bishop of Lincoln, into the Church of England.

My parents came and visited me several times, staying at the White Hart Hotel in Windsor. I remember having lunch with them there with Francis.L.Sullivan, the actor who played Jaggers in David Lean's film of Great Expectations. Another time my mother went to the performance of the two princesses in pantomime at Windsor Castle. Talking of pantomime, I vividly remember 'Jack and the Beanstalk' at the Lyceum. The giant's legs took the whole height of the proscenium arch! Another play I saw as a child was Twelfth Night at Drury Lane with a young Lawrence Olivier as Toby Belch.

Travelling to North Wales, changing at Crewe, was always an ordeal because the names of stations were blacked out, and I was carrying my 'cello in the crowded train. My father would meet me at Talsarnau junction, or Harlech, and I was always happy to be at home again, with the animals, Judy the cocker who had puppies called Bella and Bogey after a family tradition of Sir Francis, Pudding and Peter the cats.

One day two evacuees arrived from London, and were put in the bedroom above mine. Unfortunately they peed on the floor, and a large patch appeared on my bedroom ceiling.. Sir Francis was not very pleased, and I think Colonel Kirkby found somewhere else for them to stay.

I was very spoilt in the holidays, and Rose the young girl with red hair who helped in the kitchen brought my breakfast to me in bed, blushing deeply. I, of course, didn't know how to talk to her, but sixty years later visiting Maes-y-Neuadd which was now a hotel, I found that Rose still worked in the house, but it was her day off: I just said hello by telephone, remembering those happy days with nostalgia.

My father and Sir Francis were beginning to be worried about my future when I left Eton, and would be called up in the draft. Was there a way of escaping military service? It was certainly not as though I myself was looking forward to it. I had been in the cadet corps, led by Geoffrey Agnew, rather improbably for the chairman of the Bond Street art gallery, but a master at Eton. Sir Francis got me to be examined by Lord Horder, the King's physician, who had treated me years before for tonsilitis, to see if

28

if there was not some way to be excused service on health grounds, although this did not seem very patriotic.

I had had severe bouts of asthma as a child, but this was not sufficient disqualification. Regretfully Horder could provide no solution. The only possibility was to be accepted at university for a course that would be acceptable as being in the national interest. Reading Mechanical Science would be such a possibility, and I duly took the QEMST exam at Cambridge, the qualifying examination for the mechanical science tripos.

I was not really good enough in this subject, and failed the exam by a small margin. Another possibility was to do an intermediate maths degree as a preparation for the Royal Artillery who needed officers qualified in ballistics. For this I would need to volunteer, and do my basic infantry training before going on to Oxford. In the end that is what I did.

Meanwhile I got into grave trouble at Peterson's and was nearly expelled for disobedience. I can't remember the circumstances, but I think it was falsely claiming to have done a 'run' when I had not. My father was very upset and wrote me a stern letter, and my old tutor from Maes-y-Neuadd also wrote to my father saying that it was all due to my hatred of games and exercise. and that I should do more sketching in the open!

However I read a great deal, and frequented Ma Brown's bookshop in the High Street, and bought the works of Dickens and Thackeray, which I still have, and Harrison Ainsworth and Walter Scott.I also subscribed to Horizon, and read my first articles about Douanier Rousseau and Balthus.

Here is the sonnet I wrote about the School Library:

> SONNET FOR SCHOOL LIBRARY.
>
> Beneath your dome, your flower-laced ornament,
> The silent-shadow'd columns hide their store:
> Here time treads dim; the weary days are spent
> Rehearsing ancient scenes, forgotten lore.
> Amid your shelves strange kingdoms rise again :
> Black figures crouch intent on dismal fears.
> The hazy moon shines through the dusty pane,
> A glass-bound witness of the shuttered years.
> Here too, beyond your brown-leaved doors, there dwell
> The roaming fancies and the dreams obscure,
> Alike enjoying the secluded spell,
> And live alone, beyond this earthly lure.
> For in the quiet volumes bound with grey
> The straying spirit never slips away.

It was published in the Eton Chronicle on March 29th 1945. A few weeks later the war in Europe ended, and we raced around the town shouting and waving. My parents and Sir Francis moved back to Radnor, and I was very happy to be back there. Later that year I left Eton, and my army service began.

3

THE ARMY and OXFORD

The war in Europe was now over, and I had left Eton, with a leaving present of Gray's Elegy dedicated by the Headmaster, and giving leaving photographs to my friends, of which alas I do not find a copy.

The next step in my youthful life was basic training with the infantry at Bodmin, in Cornwall, as a prelude to the mathematics (intermediate) degree at Christ Church which Sir Francis had managed to arrange for me.

As Newton Ferrers was on the way to Cornwall I went to stay at Waydown with my mother and grandparents. My father had been in the army, but my grandfather was in the Fleet Air Arm which later became the Royal Air Force, and he, with another colleague, were the first men to try out the new uniform walking around Hyde Park. He also worked with the dangerous dirigibles.

In mid-August 1945 I took the train from Plymouth to Bodmin, but rather unfortunately my mother came with me. This was not really a good idea! One of the reports from Eton said that I had led a sheltered life, and that was only too true. When I got to our hut in the barracks I was with boys whom I could scarcely understand, and looking back it was the first time in my life I had come into contact with working-class boys. They were at a disadvantage never having been away from home, and very lonely.

However, after a day or two I was moved to another hut with the boys who were also going on to Oxford in six weeks' or two months' time. I was in a bunk below another boy, or perhaps I should say man, who had been to the company dentist and had all his teeth pulled out. I refused dental treatment and was marched up to the company commander and asked why. I said I had a dentist in London. He asked me what I would do if I were stationed in the middle of the desert, and I said 'I'm not, am I?' He took this in fairly good part but I seem to remember I had some punishment.

We slept on straw palliasses, and were awakened at 6 am by the bugle

My company at Bodmin, MacDonnell and Muirhead in the centre, myself on the extreme left.

calling reveille.

We were issued boots which were filled with hot oil before we went on route marches. The boots adapted perfectly to our feet! We began infantry training with lectures, PT, assault courses, drill on the square from a Guards Sergeant Major, and bayonet practice. This last was extremely violent as we had to shout as we dug the bayonets at the run into hanging sacks of straw., which we had to imagine as human bodies.

I got on well with the other men in our hut. I did my best to keep my locker tidy, and face up to the difficult exercises. Bodmin was near to get out to in the evenings, I think there was a 'British Restaurant', a standard place during the war, and I went to discover Restormel castle with a friend, Muirhead, passing by Llanhydrock Park where haymakers were loading a haywain, a scene that seemed to have come from a novel of Hardy. The castle, what there was of it, was a good destination for our walk, and I wrote a sonnet about it which was published in Country Life.

Another time we hitched a ride in a post-office van towards the coast, Wadebridge, and I remember a farm with ducks and chickens also seeming to come from the last century.

We had weekend leave, and I took the train to Plymouth to see my mother and grandmother at Newton Ferrers. I arrived at Waydown, and was shocked that there was no one there, as I had only a few coins and the house was locked. I waited anxiously, but they eventually turned up, not having received my letter-card.

Another problem was an infection in my left eye. As my right eye was extremely short-sighted, and my left eye swollen up, I couldn't see to go on parade. I was confined to our barrack-room until the swelling subsided. We were waiting from day to day for the War Office to tell us when we were due to go to Oxford, and finally the day came in October 1945.

There was one other cadet, Pennack, at Christ Church, who was lodged in New Buildings, and I was in Meadow Buildings looking towards the river. My Tutor was Dr Dundas, in Lewis Carroll's old quarters, and for Mathematics the Rev. Mascall. The others were all at different colleges, and we met up at the OTC headquarters for our gunnery and ballistics training. This was a good deal more relaxed life than Bodmin.

Meanwhile my parents and Sir Francis had settled back again at Radnor. Wisp Granville and his wife came to lunch but I had ideas about the Royal Family being only figureheads, and went to sit in a field while this important invitation took place. However when Jamie and Mary came to see us we played croquet on the lawn, and I went for walks with Mary.

Our neighbours in the house opposite, Holmbury House, were Ernest Guinness and his wife Clothilde. He was chairman of the Guinness stout company, and he employed 21 staff at the house, as well as a home farm with Guernsey cows, of which we bought the very creamy milk.

Ernest Guinness was mad on gadgets, doors opening with a photo-cell, a record player which changed the records (78s of course,) and turned them over, and a helicopter that landed in the gardens. His three daughters also visited us, Aileen, Maureen and Oonagh.

Below Radnor was another big house, Lukyns, belonging to Sir

Radnor from the air

Neville Whiethurst, Sir Francis and my father at Radnor

Kenneth Lee, Chairman of Tootal Broadhurst and Lee, cotton manufacturers, especially of Viyella shirts. He had married an American opera singer, and they entertained on quite a grand scale. They had tennis courts, and a fair amount of land which could be seen from Radnor. His nephew, Jimmy King lived nearby, and was the father of the rock impresario Jonathan King.

After Sir Francis returned from North Wales he did not venture far from Radnor, and became considerably more eccentric in his ways, keeping a Purdey gun by his bed in the case of intruders, and becoming obsessive about wasps, carrying a fly swatter with him in the summer. He had a new manservant whom he suspected of drinking his whisky, and marked the decanter upside down to find out. The Stock family were still in the servants' quarters, and their daughter, Edith, did the cleaning. Sir Francis entertained Sir Ernest Guinness's wife Clothilde to tea, I suppose when Ernest was in Ireland (he died in 1949).

At Oxford my lifelong admiration for Lewis Carroll was greatly enhanced living in his college, and I read all the material I could find about him.

I skipped many lectures, and did not do well in Physics, and at the same time had to do Officers' Training in Artillery on the Iffley Road. I also practised my 'cello, and sang the Messiah now as a bass at the Town Hall, having previously sung it both as treble and alto.

One day, high up in Meadow Buildings, I had an unexpected visitor: Lord Wilfred Greene, the Master of the Rolls, a very learned judge who lived near us at Joldwynds, Holmbury St. Mary. He was a very brilliant and charming man who was a great classicist and during the war encouraged people to save their documents from the air-raids. I was very flattered that he would climb all those stairs to see me. I think he must have been a member of the House (as Christ Church is called.)

Another contemporary was David Carritt, the art historian and director of Artemis, fine art dealers. Many years later I bumped into him at an arcade in Knightsbridge, while looking into a gallery window. By chance I had a photograph of a Siennese Madonna and Child in my wallet, which had belonged to Sir Francis. Carritt looked at it and said 'This is the Benedetto di Giovanni Madonna from the Harland Peck collection.' I was of course amazed at his visual memory. Later in fact the painting was ascribed to Fungai and sold to Agnews at Christies'.

I cannot say I made a great many friends at Oxford, apart of course from my army colleagues. Most of my Eton friends were in the army elsewhere, and others I sometimes saw them in London: James Coats, Martin Evans, and Michael Straker. I bicycled around the town, I bought a Lewis Carroll stamp case in the Turl, I suppose part of Carroll's original stock. I did however manage to do some drawing at the Ashmolean Museum, from plaster casts of classical statues, which was quite useful, and I went to the Playhouse theatre quite often.

The following year I was back in the army, posted to Field Artillery at Larkhill in the middle of Salisbury plain. We had the usual Guards Sergeant-Major for drill, and serious manoeuvres with 25 pounder guns. For this we had to learn to drive the trucks to pull the guns, both two ton trucks and 15 cwt. vehicles. My knowledge of the internal combustion engine was minimal, and my truck often stalled and we had to get it going with a starting handle. One thing I remember on these outings were the Wiltshire lardy cakes that we stopped for on the way. Delicious! I had one unfortunate experience when I drew my gun up pointing 180 degrees in the wrong direction!

Madonna and Child by Fungai

I went for a long-distance run several times with my friend Muirhead, passing close by to Stonehenge, something that could not be done today. Otherwise more artillery training, nights on guard duty outside the vehicle shed, three hours on, and three hours kip.

My group were all to go on to officer training, having passed our WOSBE, War Office Selection Board Exam. This was a sort of reality show where a dozen of us were put through our paces, the prime object being to show leadership qualities. In turn we had to instruct the other men to raise a flagpole, for example, or other tasks, as well as round-table discussions, and psychiatric evaluations. I had been told that when asked 'Why do you want to become an officer?' the appropriate answer was : 'I believe that is the best way I can serve my country!' At any rate in my case this worked, and I was ready to go to the OCTU (officers' training unit) with my other friends.

As it turned out, it did not work that way. On one of my weekend leaves to Radnor I fell ill with digestive problems. Doctor Isambard Hawes from Cranleigh was called (a descendant of the great Brunel) and I was also found to have Leukopenia, a shortage of white blood corpuscles, and I sent a note from Dr Hawes to the camp commandant, and was excused returning to duty. This lasted more than a month, and when I eventually returned to Larkhill I found most of my equipment missing, as well as my friends who had now passed on to OCTU.

The commandant was quite understanding, and put me in a hut with Polish soldiers who were mostly on barrack room duties: collecting litter and cleaning the latrines. Having nothing much to do, and being in a sort of limbo, I made myself useful at the Education Centre. There I designed posters for the weekly dances, and cleaned up the dirty glasses the day afterwards. In charge of the centre was a Sergeant -Major in the AEC, or Army Education Corps, a larger than life personality who I think was related to the Walls family, of the sausages and ice cream.

I made friends also with Michael Banks who I saw later in life when I lived in South Kensington. He advised me to join the Education Corps, and I gave up all hope of being an officer in the Gunners, and became a Sergeant in charge of the troops' education.

This was much more congenial, and I was posted to Bordon in Hampshire, where a REME unit was garrisoned. There I gave readings from T.S.Eliot, played gramophone records, arranged domestic science courses for the WACs, or women soldiers. The commanding officer at Bordon was Anthony Blond, a school friend, later a publisher, and he was astonished to see me as a sergeant in the AEC.

There were two rather unpleasant factors at Bordon. One was the Sergeants' Mess, which was run by the Catering Corps and I was expected to eat enormous amounts of sliced meat which I vomited soon after lunch every day. So instead I had tomato sandwiches at the Sally Ann, or Salvation Army Canteen.

My other problem was teaching the children of the other sergeants and soldiers. They formed a big class, very difficult to control, especially as they knew their fathers held a superior rank to mine! I managed to scare them pretending to be a ghost in a ruined house in the garrison.

In early 1947 Sir Francis, my godfather, died at Radnor. He had been ill for some time, and died of pneumonia. He was buried in the family vault at Winkfield in Berkshire, and asked that cards and a 'label set' I had made for him be put in his coffin. He left the greater part of his estate to my father, who was heartbroken at his death, but had my mother to console him.

'Goffie' did a lot for me, and loved me a lot. I never felt a great warmth for him, as I did for my grandfather, but I could not but be grateful to him for his advice (which I often did not take) and his appreciation of me and what he thought of as my rebellious nature.

This last was scarcely true, except perhaps intellectually. At that stage in my life I was quite shy, and not very courageous about leaving my home and family. However the avant-garde in art and literature excited me enormously, and I could not get enough information about Picasso, the Surrealists, and reading the magazine 'Horizon' also broadened my outlook on literature and exhbitions which I was able to visit when on leave from the army. My grandfather also encouraged me in this independent outlook.

My father's mother had died before the war, in 1939, and he did not retain many ties to his Scottish roots. He now had the responsibility of dealing with William Harland and Son, and the huge house in Belgrave Square. He was not a talented businessman, but managed to get the company back on its feet after being turned over to manufacturing camouflage paint during the war. Harlands still retained a Royal Warrant for varnish for the royal coaches, but times were changing, and the new synthetic varn-

My Scottish grandmother

iishes were replacing the formulae, often secret, used by the old varnish makers. My father made several innovations in the company: he appointed an industrial chemist, Mr. Starr, to do analyses with a spectrometer, and titrations, and he built a canteen for the work force of about thirty men.

He abandoned going up to Merton in the Rolls Royce, and bought a smaller less conspicuous car. He much preferred talking to the old varnish makers like Mr. Siviour than dealing with the office work with the company secretary, Jack Benson. He used to say he would like to throw all the papers in the air.

Meanwhile I was posted to Buchanan Castle, near Drymen, which was near Glasgow and Loch Lomond. This was the Education Corps headquarters, and I was to take the equivalent of a teachers' training course before being commissioned. The curious thing in the AEC was that the sergeants did all the teaching, and the officers (Anthony Burgess was one of them) had only administrative duties.

The course seemed to me to be very artificial as we had to pretend to be teaching our other colleagues. However after a month or two I passed satisfactorily, and was duly commissioned. There followed an embarrassing incident: a Brigadier from the War Office arrived to give us our postings: 'Smith, you are going to Korea. Robinson, you are off to Germany. Russell.....ah yes, I met your mother last week. What a charming woman! You will be posted to London.' Everyone turned to look at me of course, but I cannot say I was unhappy at my mother's intervention.

I was back at Radnor for Christmas, and went up again to the castle taking the night train from Euston to Glasgow. William Harland had an office in West Regent Street, run by a Mr. Stewart the Scottish representative who lived in Bearsden, and I often changed into 'civvies' in his office before spending a weekend leave in Glasgow, and going to the pictures, or Kelvingrove Art Gallery which had an astonishing portrait by Sargent which intrigued me.

At the castle there were three or four other second-lieutenants who, like me, were to be posted to Eltham in London . I was given 226 service clothing coupons, and a room to myself. It was extremely cold, but there was a slow-burning stove in the room.

I was put in charge of 'G' Platoon, consisting of syndicates of trained teachers

Buchanan Castle after the war

and graduates. I was glad I was not going through the absurd teachers' course again! The only advantage being that it qualified as a diploma in Civvy Street if ever I wanted to teach as a profession.

I finally left Buchanan Castle in the first days of January 1948, spending a while in Glasgow, and then back to my new posting at Eltham Palace, which was the headquarters of the RAEC. I shared a room with another officer, and had a batman for the first time to bring me early morning tea. Not being a tea drinker this was not a great privilege.

The days mostly consisted of lectures in subjects like 'British Way and Purpose', but in the evenings I often went into London to see my parents who were staying in South Kensington, and I went to the cinema and concerts. I also caught up with a dear schoolfriend from Eton: James Coats, who was now living in Thurloe Square, and had dinner with his family. He was starting a term at the Old Vic, having aspirations to be an actor.

Somehow I fitted a lot of reading into my life, especially Henry James, at the time, and I also went to the West End galleries. The army also organised some visits, for example to the Siemens factory where we saw radar for the first time on the roof. Towards the end of January I heard that I had been posted to headquarters, London Disrict, which turned out to be the Guards and Household Brigade, with its headquarters at Palace Court in Bayswater.

Here I met John Herrington, an affable aspiring actor, and a number of Education Corps officers. My job was to supervise classes at the various London barracks, and it has to be said that the soldiers were in need of very elementary education in the three Rs. But also I had to cope with a great deal of form filling, indenting: the army's bureaucracy.

Visiting Chelsea Barracks, Wellington barracks, and Knightsbridge barracks. At Wellington I saw my school friend Michael Straker. There were several Old Etonians on the mess balcony looking down at me as I arrived in my new and very smart Education Corps uniform. And of course the sentries at Buckingham Palace had to salute as I went past.

At Chelsea barracks I had been boxing when at Gibbs's, and now I believe the site is to be developed into a housing complex on a grand scale.

In the midst of my military activities I would go up and down to Radnor by train, often with Anthony Touche, and spend the weekends at home painting, or in the garden. In London I seem to have gone to the cinema or theatre, or concerts, most evenings. I am now consulting eight years of very complete Collins page-a-day diaries which I have not looked at for many years. The diaries are very factual, not at all expressing emotions, just my day-to-day activities. Which in fact is more useful for writing these memoirs.

The appointment to HQ London District did not last very long, and at the end of April I was posted to Feltham, west of London. A captain Sallabank showed me around the education quarters. I had a sergeant, a corporal and woman secretary in the office which was in a mess that I did not feel like clearing up. Most days before lunch Sallabank would phone me and ask me to come and have a 'snifter' or drink.

As usual I supervised classes, but spent most of the days reading the newspaper: the education office was not a hive of activity. I had a course at Chatham House in St.James's Square, and lunch at Stewarts, the tearooms on the corner of Piccadilly and Bond Street. This was a simple and good place on two floors. My mother knew all the waitresses and would get a good table when she went there!

Every day I took the train down to Dorking, and Thurston the taxi would meet me to go to Radnor, about nine miles west. At the weekends I would paint, and if I had time in London would visit the Bond Street galleries and often eat at the National Book League. My father belonged to the Royal Thames Yacht Club although he hated the sea and sailing: it was just convenient when we lived in Sloane Street, being near the French Embassy in Knightsbridge. He asked me if I wanted to join, but I was not keen.

Before being demobilised we were allowed a month of training for a civilian job, and I opted to go to Harlands, though I did not foresee a life in the paint works. However it was interesting to see the different sides of the industry, the laboratory, the paint mixers, the offices. I worked with the spectrometer and did titrations, but I could see that the old methods of varnish and paint making were on their way out. I designed some labels and brochures: 'Harlands, The Peak of Perfection'!

At the beginning of July I heard that my release instructions had come through. My release book was made out at the Horseguards. However I had a few more days teaching the army bandsmen at Kneller Hall in Twickenham.

I paid my mess bill, said goodbye to Captain Sallabank, and on the 10th of July went to Aldershot by train from Guildford to be demobbed. Sweet rations and civilian clothes, shoes that seemed to be made of cardboard.

Sunday July 11th, my first day out

AEC button and cap badge

of the army, and I found it difficult to believe. I now had to get down to work on my painting, a desire I had been waiting for a long time. Although perhaps my father had other ideas for me, for example law or politics, he never wanted to influence me in my choice of a career, and of course my grandfather was very happy that I would be following in his footsteps.

The day I left the army David Lutyens my schoolfriend from Eton came down to Radnor for the day with his mother.

David was a small man with an immense forehead crowned by curly hair, and a sensual mouth and melancholy eyes. To see him at the typewriter was extraordinary: the sheets of paper emerged like a torrent with poetry and plays. In fact I still have a poem he wrote that day, thanking me for a day's outing in the country.

David was the grandson of the great architect Edwin Lutyens, and great grandson of Edward Bulwer Lytton, author of 'The Last Days of Pompeii'. His father Robert was also an architect, and his mother was a Polish *Grande Dame* who had set up a dressmaking business in their house in Palace Street near Buckingham Palace. She was rumoured to have introduced Edward, the Prince of Wales, to Mrs. Simpson who was one of her customers.

In years to come I saw a lot of this eccentric and brilliant writer, but not always under the happiest of circumstances.

David Russell 'The Card Players', oil on canvas, 1978

4

ART SCHOOL and TRAVEL

Back at Radnor, as well as painting every day, I played the piano. I had swapped my Challen baby grand for a Steinberg which belonged to a family friend, Leslie Murray-Aynsley. He was going to Jamaica for the British Council and the Challen would resist the tropical climate better.

An important family event after I left the army was the conversion of the mews house at 9 Belgrave Square Mews North, adjoining the huge house in the square. This was an excellent pied-à-terre for my parents and myself, near Sloane Street where we had lived before the war, and Butler the chauffeur-gardener would come up from Radnor with fruit and vegetables from the garden, and the mail.

My life in the years following the army were very much devoted to painting, music, reading, and the garden. Looking back I can see that this quite hermetic life was to a degree cowardly: I did not strike out on my own socially and I accepted my parents' style of life and friends. My first ventures abroad were with them. First with my mother staying in a private flat on the Boulevard Berthier in Paris: an old lady and her maid who served boiled potatoes as a separate course after the meat. But I saw the Louvre and went sight-seeing.

I had my 21st birthday on 15th June 1948 and my father gave me a gold watch and a cheque, and in the evening we went to the theatre to see 'Four Five Six' with Bobby Howes and Binnie Hale, and then dinner at Prunier's.

In August we went to Gothenburg in Sweden on the 'Saga', a boat from Tilbury, to stay with great friends Hoagy and Tora Turitz. They had two children, Claes and Ian about my age, and a house by the sea at Saro, and a magnifent apartment in Gothenburg. Hoagy who was Norwegian, owned the big department store Ferna Lundquist, now NK, as well as a splendid collection of impressionist paintings, including Cezanne, Renoir and Monet.

Tora was from Malmö, and the whole family was mad on the sea. We went fishing for mackerel, and nearly as far as Denmark in Hoagy's motor yacht. Claes later won the Swedish gold cup for yacht racing.

A guest at the house in Saro was M. Pellerin, the son of Auguste who had an enormous collection of Cezannes. I think he was resident in Sweden, but we spoke in French and played rummy after a dinner with a lot of 'skals!'

We went on to Stockholm for three days, dining at the Gyldene Freden restaurant, the cellar of an old house where the Swedish composer Bellman had played, and Anders Zorn lived, and then going to see 'Il Barbiere' at the opera with Tito Gobbi. The days seem crammed with activity looking at my diary, but as tourists it is amazing how much can be done in a few days. We also had dinner at Bellmansro, with a quartet playing in period costume.

We went to the National Museum where there were paintings from Vienna including Vermeer's 'The Artist Painting' from the Kunsthistorisches Museum. On the 16th. September we were back in Tilbury.

My life at Radnor consisted of painting every day in my studio, self-portraits, still lives, exploring different techniques and styles. I read a lot of art history, and had a great passion for Picasso. The wireless held an important place in my life: the Brains Trust, Round Britain Quiz, Itma.

My grandparents were now living in Torquay: a flat in 'The Terrace' overlooking the harbour. It was a small flat belonging to a Miss Pinney, above a solicitor's. But my grandfather had a studio in the 'Upper Terrace,' a delightful place in a small courtyard, now sadly demolished. His relations with my grandmother were not of the happiest. I have bundles of his letters he wrote to my mother about her intransigeant behaviour: objecting to him going out for a drink with his friend Sean O'Casey who lived nearby, and even going up to his studio with her sister Jessie to 'tidy up', which sometimes meant putting away objects from a still-life that he was working on. I believe that in fact my grandmother never really forgave my grandfather for becoming a painter rather than a respectable engineer.

In September my mother and I went down to Torquay for a show we were all exhibiting in, in Plymouth.

Tora, Marjorie, Myself and Hoagy at Saro

In those days I also wrote a lot of poetry which I had lost until recently. I had something in the Poetry Review. I also planned a children's book which never got finished.

In October 1948 I and my parents went to Amsterdam via Harwich and the Hook of Holland. Being extremely enamoured of Rembrandt this was a very exciting visit for me. Seeing the 'Night Watch' at the Rijksmuseum was the most enthralling encounter with a painting I had ever had: it reduced me to tears. I was also lucky on this trip as there were exhibited also masterpieces from the Munich Pinacotek, including the Rubens 'Rape of the Sabine Women.'

Otherwise I went to the Stedelijk Museum, the Rembrandthuis, and the Jan Six house. After staying at the Amstel Hotel we went to the Hague and the Mauritshuis with the superb Vermeers, a huge Paul Potter, and Rembrandt self-portrait. At that time all very badly lit.

The next stop was Brussels, by train, where we stayed with Margaret Kingsley and her daughter. Charles and Margaret were great friends, Charles being a descendant of the writer, and a stockbroker who invented the 'chart' for share prices. We did the usual tourist round, including the Musée Moderne, the Musée Royale, and especially the Musée Wiertz whose work reminded me of Füssli in its morbid iconography.

Having had so many years of rationing in England the sight of bananas and other things we had not eaten for years was tremendous. We also had marvellous 'frites' as only the Belgians can cook them at Margaret's house, and before leaving bought two kilos of chocolates at Godiva in the Chaussée de Charleroi. I also bought an anatomical plaster horse which I have to this day. We returned to London via Ostend and Dover.

In December the London house was nearly ready, and we stayed at the Tudor Court Hotel in South Kensington while the gas was connected, and carpets laid. One evening I went to the Classic cinema in Chelsea to see 'Les Enfants du Paradis' with Erika Brausen from the Hanover Gallery, where later I was to have my first show in London.

Antoine Wiertz: La Belle Rosine 1847

David Russell: My studio at Radnor, oil on canvas

During the rest of the year I painted nearly every day in my studio, which had been the kitchen of the house in past times. It is in the centre of the painting on the left. I was very experimental, if that is the right word, still lives, portraits, imagined subjects, often painting over canvases and using them again. In November I painted a still life with kitchen scales, (below right,) and submitted work at the RI galleries in London without success.

    Towards the end of the year I went to Chelsea Art School for an interview with Harold Williamson, the Head of the school. He liked my work (I took several different things, portrait, drawings etc. to show him.) and said I could start in the next term. I was happy about this, as I also had three school friends studying there, Mason, Chinnery and Rossiter.

    The Belgrave Mews flat was coming along, and I hired an upright piano, and brought up painting materials from Radnor. One weekend on my own I had my first real sexual encounter with a girl from Shepherds' Market. I was nervous and inexperienced, but also excited, and she led me along in a sympathetic way. Later I frequented, if that's the right word, a French girl in a house off Curzon Street, who gave me tips about good cheap places to eat in Paris.

    My parents had become friendly with David Webster, the General Administrator of Covent Garden Opera House, and his partner Jimmy Belle. Webster invited us to the dress rehearsal of the ballet 'Cinderella' with Frederick Ashton, Moira Shearer and Michael Soames. The next day we went to the première, and met Graham Sutherland, Oliver Messel, and Hardy Amies at dinner. Going home we saw the Christmas lights in Trafalgar Square. The next day was Christmas Eve and we bought a puppy.

Still life with scales 1948, oil on canvas

In January of 1949 I started my course at Chelsea Art School. I mainly worked in the life room, and the teachers were Ceri Richards, an exhuberant Welshman, Claude Rogers a more timid soul with a beard, of the Euston Road group, and Edward Wakeford. Henry Moore taught sculpture, and Prunella Clough also taught there, although I do not remember meeting her until much later.

I was quite confused between the teaching styles of Richards and Rogers. Ceri Richards would draw on the edge of my pad in swirling curves, aiming to emphasise the rounded nature of the model's limbs. I was trying to emulate this technique, but then it would be a morning with Rogers whose idea was to look for significant points on the body, and then join them up, rather like a child's joining -up -the- numbers drawing. The problem was that I worked fast, and had probably done a dozen sketches by the time the master came around. I cannot say I learnt a great deal.

We had a marvellously professional Italian model, an old man whose family had been models for generations. There was also an ex-boxer who took a fighting attitude if a student came too near. This was all good practice, and I worked in pencil, in conté and Indian ink.

In May there was a break from school: we went to Paris with my mother and grandparents. For my grandfather it was a great experience, his first visit to France after a lifetime of admiring the French painters, Impressionists onwards. We went to lunch at Chez Francis in the Place de l'Alma and he got out his sketchbook and did some delightful drawings of the café tables. We did all the usual sights, the Louvre, the Orangerie, the Invalides. Lunch at Armenonville, taxi to Versailles. At the restaurant Le Catalan in rue des Grands Augustins, near Picasso's studio, we had lunch and did drawings in the visitors' book which had sketches by Picasso, Braque, and surprisingly Lucien Freud and John Craxton. We stuck to the English habit of afternoon tea at Ladurée, Weber, or Rumpelmeyer. Otherwise the Salon des Independants and Pierre Loeb, Durand Ruel and others.

My stint at Chelsea School lasted about six months, but I felt it wasn't getting me anywhere useful, and continued painting at Radnor every day, except for excursions to London when my father would drop me at Wimbledon station before going on to the works at Merton.

We now had a French cook at Radnor: Madame Bossy. A motherly type with dyed red hair from Montmartre. She made vol-au-vents, croissants, millefeuilles and countless other delicious things. My father took her to London every Tuesday for her day off, and she sent packets of real coffee to her family in France who were surviving on chicory substitute.

45

During the summer of 1949 I worked hard in my studio at Radnor, trying new styles, influenced by various painters, and especially Picasso. But I also strived to do academic portraits and still lives, with some limited success.

About once a week I would go to London with my father, and borrow books from Harrods' lending library, and go round the exhibitions. Erika Brausen had a show of Francis Bacon at the Hanover, and nine out of twelve were sold for prices between £150 and £250.

There was no television yet, and I listened a lot to the radio: music and programmes like 'Round Britain Quiz' and 'The Brains Trust'. The critic Eric Newton on Sundays. I played croquet on the lawn with my mother, and backgammon and chess. My great enthusiasm for gardening had not yet begun, though I bought a load of stone for a rockery to the west of the house.

In July may parents and I went down to Beaulieu to a house, Littlemarsh, that David Webster had rented from the musician Etienne Amyot, the originator of the BBC Third Programme of classical music. There we made a great friend, the pianist Clive Lythgoe. David Webster had been quite scathing about an after-dinner performance he gave of Liszt's Mephisto Waltz, and my father, feeling sorry for Clive, walked by the sea with him to reassure him, and a great friendship grew from that evening.

I never met Amyot, but his neighbour was Lord Montagu, a schoolfriend, who had been sent by his parents to Canada for part of the war, but came back to Eton before the war ended. There is a classic interview of Edward Montagu and Amyot in the BBC archives.

In September another big trip with my parents, this time to Italy which I had been longing to see. On the 18th we took the usual Golden Arrow train to Paris and stayed at the Castiglione Hotel in the Faubourg St. Honoré. Madame Bossy was also on holiday and had left us flowers at the hotel, and came for a drink. I saw de Sica's 'Bicycle Thieves' at the Madeleine cinema, and we took a sleeper to Milan and then Venice.

I had often dreamed of Venice, and when I saw the Canal Grande I recognised it, as well as Piazza San Marco. We stayed at the Danieli and saw de Chirico in the lounge. We went to the Fenice to see Goethe's 'Iphigenia in Tauris' and had tea at Quadri and Florian.

On to Florence at the Excelsior for three days, which included a communist parade with banners of Togliatti, and the Uffizi. On to Rome at the Grand Hotel where we picked up money in Italian currency by courtesy of a Mr Tobolski in London who had an Italian agent (at that time there were heavy restrictions on exporting currency from the UK.)

After Rome we went up to stay at Santa Margherita Ligure, then a pleasant small seaside town before all the construction work had started. As it was the end of the season we had a quiet stay at the Albergo Imperiale, and the chef would ask us each morning what we would like to eat: we were the only guests in the huge hotel!

On to Genoa by bus, and the Palazzo Bianco, and the Hanbury gardens at La Mortola. After that Vence, the Picasso Museum in Antibes, and back to Paris. There we met Ian Turitz who was working at the Swedish Institut Tessin, and we had dinner at the Grand Vatel and tea at Les Cascades.

We had been away about a month. Butler met us at Victoria, and Madame Bossy was also back from her holiday.

Italy had a great effect on me, and although I had come to admire the intimacy and taste of the French, perhaps the architectural strength and the Mediterranean spirit excited me more. In any case this visit changed my ideas and eventually my life. It certainly showed up in my painting.

Sadly, after all the effort of decorating and furnishing the house in Belgrave Mews North, my father decided to sell the main house, 9 Belgrave Square. The problem was that because of its huge size the local taxes were enormous, and as I remember it was sold by Knight, Frank and Rutley for the, today, ridiculous sum of £4000. There had been damage during the war, and my father could not afford to keep it. It became the headquarters of the Institute of Directors. and my father looked in from time to time, remembering the days of Mrs. Harland Peck.

The cost of heating Radnor in the winter was also becoming prohibitive, and my father started looking for a furnished flat in London for the winter. He eventually found one at Dalmeny House in the Brompton Road, opposite the Oratory.

Croquet on the lawn at Radnor

Covent Garden Programme

We all moved up to South Kensington, including Madame Bossy, and I took a small easel and colours with me. We visited Douglas Cooper at 18 Egerton Terrace, the Australian collector and friend of Picasso, who was staying at Lord Amulree's house with his friend John Richardson. Cooper's collection of Picasso's cubist period was stunning. Cooper and Richardson visited us at Dalmeny House, and I showed them my paintings, which met with approval in spite of my debt, at the time, to de Chirico.

I also went to the Tate opening of the Fernand Leger exhibition, and met the great man himself, rather gruff and silent.

I had some sort of routine in London, often having lunch at the 'Cordon Rouge' in Sloane Street, visiting the London Library, and ordeing a new suit at Denman and Godard. On 9th March there was a State Performance at Covent Garden for President Auriol of France. We took Madame Bossy to see the King and Queen, and Princess Elizabeth and the Auriols. Churchill came after a division in the House at 10pm.

The ballet programme included Symphonic Variations with Fonteyn and Shearer, and Façade, and the last act of The Sleeping Beauty. We talked to David Webster and his partner Jimmy Belle, and saw Osbert and Sacheverell Sitwell. I illustrate the programme designed by Oliver Messel.

I bought a zither. As in the twenties the ukelele had been the fashionable instrument, so with Anton Karas's playing in 'The Third Man', the zither became the instrument of the fifties. However, it was difficult to play, and difficult to get strings. I had the 'Café Mozart' sheet music, and managed to achieve a very modest success.

In March it was back to Radnor, and in April.....a TV aerial! This was to change my habit of listening to music on the radio, and though still in black and white, it was a big improvement on the set I had seen in 1937 at Neville Whitehurst's house in Weybridge.

We took Madame Bossy to the Derby, but later in the year she decided to go back to France, and we missed all those éclairs and mille-feuilles. As well as her formidable and authoritative presence. And in spite of her sudden decisions to go to Montmartre for the weekend.

Friends of my parents, Lord Justice Hilberry and his wife came to stay, with bodyguards and detectives stationed outside the house. He was hearing a case concerning the troubles in Ireland.

There were now three generations of cats living in the gardens at Radnor: Swisher, the little tabby, Queenie her half-Persian daughter, and Kitty her grandson, a black-and-white tom, and my own pet. I painted Kitty in various styles, and made birthday or Christmas cards with his countenance.

Very sadly Swisher was run over in the autumn of 1950, and many years later Kitty suffered the same fate after he had been on the tiles for some days.

In September 1950 we took the Golden Arrow once again to Paris, and stayed at the Oxford and Cambridge Hotel. We had lunch at the W.H.Smith's restaurant upstairs in the rue de Rivoli, now sadly gone, and saw the Matisse cutouts at the Maison de la Pensée Française.

Images of Kitty

The next day we took the bus heading south, staying the night at St. Etienne, then down through Montelimar and Orange, with lunch at Avignon. We arrived at Nice late in the evening, and stayed one night at the Hotel Albert I..

In the following days we visited Monte Carlo, and had lunch at the Scottish Tearooms in Nice. Then my mother fell ill and was taken to the Queen Victoria Hospital on the way to Villefranche. My father and I took the bus to visit her for several days. She had made friends with Lady Anson who was a fellow patient, and seemed to be quite happy staying on in the hospital which had good food served outside on the tyerrace.

I lost some money at the Nice Casino, and the day after my father and I went to stay in Biot, in the hills behind Antibes. A charming village, and a little hotel, the 'Jarres d'Or.'

I did a lot of gouaches in Biot: the little hotel had a garden where I could work. We visited the pottery in Biot, and the Fragonard Museum in Grasse. After three weeks in France, my mother having recovered, we returned on the Golden Arrow again, and Butler picked us up as usual at the station.

We went down to Torquay to see my grandparents in November, and my mother and I both painted portraits of my grandfather, (see illustration no. ii.) and I was pleased with mine. My grandfather often saw Sean O'Casey, who was a neighbour, at the local pub.

etching on zinc, 1952

1951 was spent painting and gardening, a new enthusiasm which I had felt was the preserve of Butler and Berridge, the gardeners at Radnor, but now I formed an interest for myself, and began to learn some botany and horticulture, and began by making a fernery, inspired by Victorian books that I had, to the west of the house, under the shade of a pine and copper beech. I joined the British Pteridological Society, the president of which was the Reverend Elliot of Reading, and I scoured the catalogues for rare plants and spores. My ambition was to grow exotic species, Musa basjoo the semi-hardy banana for example which I had seen at Nymans, and the Chinese fan palm, Trachycarpus fortunei. These sorts of foliage plants are much in demand today, but in the 1950s were a great rarity except in some Cornish gardens.

But I also transplanted many shrubs and other plants from parts of the garden north of the house, where Lady Granville had made a pond with royal ferns and primulas in a clay surround. There was also a large patch of bluebells and a sloping field which we called 'Scotland' because of its hillocks and damp atmosphere. This led down to another pond where moorhens bred, next to Sherborne Lane, a bridle path which went through our property towards the village of Ewhurst, supposedly a route for smugglers from the coast in past times.

The stream which fed these two ponds meandered to a further pond at the bottom of the gardens, and this I enlarged with rocks and a waterfall, and planted Gunnera manicata in a sort of dell near the pond, which I will illustrate in a later photograph. Further up the hill I decided to construct a 'temple' (see the photograph on the next page.)

I built this myself, with hardly any help. I made the columns by pouring cement into rolls of linoleum left over from the house, and reinforced with pieces of iron fencing no longer used. The dome was made also with iron struts covered with bamboo and cemented. I had intended to paint the ceiling inside with a fresco, but never got down to it. In the aerial view of Radnor on page 32 it can be seen at the far left of the photograph.

In May Erika Brausen from the Hanover Gallery came down to see my work, and was impressed, and said she would give me a show 'when I was ready'. I did not in fact feel that I was, but was very excited at the thought that I might exhibit in such a prestigious gallery..

In many ways my life was restricted in these years to gardening and paintoing. and my social life was largely that of my parents. My father would drive up to work at Merton and drop me off at Wimbledon tube station, from where I would go to Sloane Square or Piccadilly. I bought colours and canvases at Lechertier Barbe in Jermyn Street, and changed books at the nearby London Library. But my main passion had become gardening, and I went to the Royal Horticultural Society's shows in Vincent Square, and collected plant and seed catalogues, and had correspondence with Mr. Shrub of Hilliers of Winchester, Marchants, Kaye's nursery for ferns, and even nurseries in New Zealand. I met Lanning Roper who worked at the RHS, and he became a good friend and encouraged me to enter a Flowering Shrub competition at Chelsea Flower Show. This was ambitious for me as competitors were some of the great English gardens like Leonardslee or Sheffield Park. However I was quite happy with my Lomaria and other shrubs, although taking such big cuttings did not exactly improve the plants!

Succeeding Madame Bossy a French boy named Camille from Normandy came down to Radnor. He was not a cook, although he made a good vegetable soup, but he helped in the kitchen and cleaning. His ambition was to be an accountant in Canada, and he did not stay long. It was not until April 1952 that my parents found a replacement: an Italian couple from Lake Garda, Bruna and Cesare Murari.

Bruna had been in service since the age of thirteen and was an excellent cook, especially of dishes from the region, like gnocchi and risotto. Cesare had been a waiter and was good at answering the door and welcoming guests, but he left most of the hard work to his wife. They had the magazine 'Oggi' sent every week, and Bruna helped me with my Italian: so far I had had no formal lessons, but I found that Latin and French helped a lot.

The Temple in summer

In August we went to Switzerland armed with Baedeker and a flora of the Alps. We took the ferry from Folkestone to Boulogne and a sleeper to Interlaken where we stayed at the Beau Rivage Hotel. I immediately went hunting for ferns and found some good specimens of Asplenium, Polypodium and Dryopteris. There was a splendid view of the Jungfrau from the hotel.

Concerts at the Kursaal, yodelling and flag-throwing. A steamer to Geissbach on Lake Brienz. Then the train to Bern and childhood memories of Mary Plain, the children's books about a little bear from the bear pits.

We took the train to the Schynige Platte with its fabulous views and alpine flowers: gentians, edelweiss, saxifrages.

Next the train to Lucerne and lunch at the Schwanen restaurant, and visit to the Old Bridge. Thence to Lugano where we stayed several days, with a trip to Ancona and Locarno. My father saw a house right on the lake for £5000, but my mother did not like lakes, but loved the sea. It would have been a great investment. I saw it again with regret many years later.

We went to the Villa Favorita at Cassarate and saw the Thyssen collection, full of extraordinary masterpieces, especially a group by Franz Hals, as well as Bosch, El Greco, and a wonderful small landscape of Rembrandt.

We went to Gandria and Menaggio, and saw ythe Villa Carlotta with the Canova sculpture of Eros and Psyche. Then to Milan where we saw the usual tourist attractions, the cathedral and Leonardo's Last Supper, as well as the Castello Sforzesco. A few years later I would be back.

Back to England and Butler meeting us with the Rolls Royce, after a few days in Paris at the Castiglione. We had been away nearly a month. The pond at Radnor had silted over and there was a lot to do in the garden.

Rose Garden at Radnor, with Temple in the distance

Our neighbours at Radnor were a Mr. Huggett at Hurtwood House, above us, and Sir Kenneth Lee, chairman of the cotton manufacturers Tootal Broadhurst and Lee, below.

Lee had entertained Joseph Kennedy at Lukyns, their big modern house to the south of Radnor. I met a number of interesting people there, including the harpist Mildred Dilling who bought two

Interior, oil on canvas, 1951

drawings of mine with musical instruments, and whom I later visited many years later in New York. She taught Harpo Marx the harp.

Opposite us Holmbury House was sold to a Maharajah, I think of Jaipur, of whom local gossip related that he had juke boxes in every room. The house was later sold to Mullard Space Laboratories who worked on satellites. Towards the end of 1951 there was a sale of furniture and garden ornaments. We bought two stone urns which can be seen on the previous page.

My horticultural efforts were not always successful. The fact was that I had had no training, and my desire to grow sub-tropical plants in the open, even with the south facing micro-climate, often ended in failure. The next year I persuaded my father to buy a small greenhouse which was built on the taerrace, attached to the east wing of the house. There I was able to protect the many tender plants and shrubs I had bought, as well as propagating them from seed and cuttings.

I was experimenting with small scuptures in plaster and metal, but also made a series of etchings (page 50) on zinc which I did not print myself, but sent them to the firm of Kimber in London. I would buy the plates from them, and then send them by post to be printed. They did an excellent job, but I did not print complete editions. Vittoria Pozzi, the master printer in Florence now has the plates.

Essentially my paintings of this period were dark (inspired I think by my love of Rembrandt) and the subjects were still lives of 'metaphysical' objects. Robert Melville, writing later in the Architectural Review, likened them to objects in an alchemist's cellar, and Gio Ponti, the architect, to the first depictions of instruments of torture in English painting! I illustrate one of these paintings above. It was painted with many layers, perhaps ten or twenty, of varnish glazes. Now, instead of buying expensive copal varnish from Lechertier Barbe, my father brought me cans of excellent synthetic varnish from Harlands. I admit that some of my own paintings gave me nightmares.

I and my father in Naples

In the autumn we took another trip, this time again to Santa Margherita and Portofino where Cesare had a friend. He had the idea of my father buying a small restaurant which Cesare would run with Bruna. My father went so far as to look at one or two places, but was put off by the idea that in some way you were not buying the walls of the place.

I always took English books to read, and this time it was Simenon in English. I also went to any nurseries I could find to buy small plants or seeds to take home.

My father was always worried about currency and relied on friends to make a delivery: eventually an Important Letter would arrive, and all would be well.

After visiting Rapallo and Genoa we took the night train to Naples, staing at the Albergo Vesuvio. We had lunch at Zi Teresa opposite, and the next day took a car to Pompeii and Sorrento. There we called at the Villa Tritone where our friend Friedl Schorr from Chelsea had friends, the Schelers, who showed us around the magnificent gardens: Strelitzias, Jacaranda, Dasylirion, nutmeg trees. Scheler said the only things he could not grow, and liked very much, were lupins!

Back in Naples we had tea at Caflisch in Via Roma, and went to the Botanic Garden where I spoke to the director. The gardens had been very neglected and damaged during the war, and only one old man knew the names of the trees and plants: the labels had been lost. The director wanted a Metasequoia glyptostroboides and I promised to send him one when I got back to England. In return he gave me small plants of Chamaedorea and the pink Bignonia, as well as a lot of palm seeds.

I went with my mother to the Museo Nazionale, with its splendid sculptures and objects from Pompeii. With a little persuasion we were allowed into the room of Erotica. My mother, to avoid my embarrassment, pretended she had left her spectacles behind and could not quite see what was going on in these images. The next day we went to Amalfi and Ravello where we saw the gardens of the Villa Ruffolo with its spectacular views, then Positano and back for dinner and a revue at the Mercadente theatre.

The next day my mother and I went to Capri, my father feeling too tired. We took a rowing boat to see the Grotta Azzurra and then the funicular up to the town and lunch at Sett'Anni. Then to Anacapri and Axel Munthe's villa San Michele, and the hotel where King Farouk was staying.

The next day I went with my father to a local varnish factory which employed about 50 people. The director took us to lunch, then to Posilippo gardens of remembrance.We also went to San Carlo Operas House to see the English Festival Ballet in Lac des Cygnes.

The next day, with my father, to Capri again, staying at the Morgana Tiberio hotel. However I caught a fever, and after a day or so we took the train to Rome, to the Mediterraneo hotel where I saw the doctor. I managed to get to the Palazzo Doria before leaving and saw the Velasquez Pope Pius which I very much admired.

Back to the Castiglione in Paris by train. I saw Victor Brauner at his show at the Galerie de France. Then Radnor where Bruna had done a lot of embroidery, handkerchiefs and tablecloth, and she and Cesare had thoroughly cleaned the house.

In September Erika Brausen from the Hanover Gallery came down again and liked the work and asked me to go to the gallery about booking a time for a show. Next time I went to London she suggested February 1954 to which of course I agreed, although it seemed a long time to wait.In the meantime I showed several paintings together with my grandfather at the Plymouth Museum, and a painting in the London Group.

5

BRIGHTON, HANOVER GALLERY and ITALY

1953 was largely spent gardening and painting. Perhaps more of the former. I ordered and planted dozens of trees, shrubs and herbaceous plants, as well as propagating from seeds and layers. It was the year of the Coronation (watched on television), and the death of Stalin.

In April Cesare and Bruna left after a year at Radnor. Cesare thought of it as a 'gilded prison', and during their trips to London had found a probably more rewarding job. I missed the excellent cooking and Italian conversation. But they were soon to be replaced by another couple from Italy, Mario Zentillin and his wife Ilesa from Friuli. But they had much less experience of running a household, and my mother had to teach them a lot.

I continued with the engravings on zinc plates with an electrical tool which gave me exactly the effect I wanted, and sent them off to Kimber to print. Looking a my diary of this year it is very difficult to identify paintings except by their size, which is how I listed them: 25" x 36", or 40" x 50" for example. I initially painted the 'dark' subjects on canvases from Roberson, but this became expensive and I used masonite or hardboard which I sawed and sealed myself. I now regret this, as the quality of the handling suffered.

It was also a year when my mother had an appendectomy and hysterectomy at a clinic in Queen's Gate, the surgeon being Mr.Reid. My father complained of digestive pains, and had a gall bladder operation in the Guildford Hospital, his progress being monitored by our local doctor, Isambard Hawes, (a descendant of Brunel.) As for me I continued to have extremely painful mouth ulcers and had to undergo barium meal tests, swallowing a tube to draw off liquid at intervals: very uncomfortable.

My father had a few weeks convalescing at the Dudley Hotel in Hove, and my mother and I also went down to see him, and thence the idea of renting a flat in Brighton or Hove for the winter months.

Our friend, the concert pianist Clive Lythgoe, was now living in Hove, in Brunswick Square. His partner was Peter James who worked in set design in the film industry, and they helped us look for a flat for the winter as my father was now finding the heating at Radnor exhorbitant.

Eventually we found a top floor flat, also in Brunswick Square, with a big balcony looking towards the sea. My father rented it for 2½ years unfurnished, and we brought furniture from Radnor as well as buying other pieces.

The flat was not large, but there was a bedroom for me, and Peter helped with the decoration: a black wallpaper with with large roses for one room only in the living-room, typical of the nineteen-fifties. I was also lucky to find a studio nearby. off the Western Road, in a courtyard. It had been a knitting factory and had a garage beneath which my father could use.

My parents: breakfast on the balcony Brunswick Square, Hove

We saw Clive and Peter most days, and a French friend of theirs, Yves, who was working in Brighton. We ate out a lot: the 'Patisserie', the 'Cordoba Café', 'Zetlands', and the excellent fish restaurants: English's, and Sweetings.

I used the Brighton Library regularly, and went up to London at least once a week, and to Radnor from time to time to look at the plants and the cats: the Butlers were still there.

In my studio in Hove

I arranged with Erika and Robert Melville to have my paintings framed by Alfred Hecht in the King's Road. They chose 14, including a very large painting on board: 'Oedipus and the Sphinx', 5' x 8' (below).

Hecht had framed the Francis Bacon paintings for the Hanover Gallery, and had a fine Bacon hanging on a black wall in his dining-room.

I was naturally very excited about this show, my first, and as well as the paintings a number of my engravings were framed in coloured mounts by Hecht, and they looked very good. I shared the gallery with Bruce Hollingsworth who showed in the smaller space upstairs.

My grandparents came up from Devon a few days before the private view of the show, and we went to the gallery the day before. The pictures looked good; the big paintings in their gold frames were impressive. That day the French ambassador, René Massigli had come in, and the sculptor F.E.McWilliam who asked me if I was interested in doing sculpture. Many old friends turned up the next day; my school friends James Coats and Oliver Evans Palmer, Clive and Peter, David Webster, and the Kingsleys. As I was leaving Sir John Rothenstein, director of the Tate came in, and I spoke to him. It seemed that he was interested in buying a picture for the Tate, but in the end did not. The prices were £50 to £100 for the biggest painting, but I sold only two. Also one to Milo Cripps, a cousin of James Coats.

I had a few good reviews in the newspapers. Robert Melville wrote in the Architectural Review that such subjects of alienation needed a more precise technique. I think he thought of me as a sort of hermit-alchemist. He came down to see my new work later in Brighton, and told my parents of a woman painter who, when she had left home after a cloistered existence, took up a life of orgies and debauchery!

There was also a good review in 'Time and Tide' by one Joseph Rykwert, whom Erika Brausen said I should certainly meet. There were certain critics, such as Eric Newton, who made a point of not meeting the subjects of their articles, for fear of bias, unlike their Italian colleagues who all promoted their pet artists.

Joseph who was a Polish Jew converted to Catholicism turned out to become a very great friend. He was an architect, and architectural historian. living in a strange 'mansarde' flat in Kingly Street, near Liberty's. He had been a student, but now was writing criticism.

Oedipus and the Sphinx, oil on board, 1953

There were beams crossing his room at waist height, and great piles of books surrounding his bed. He later lived in a shop in Hampstead and could be seen writing through the shop window.

Life went on in Brighton, seeing Clive and Peter most days, and going to Clive's recitals and concerts, or hearing him play at home on his Broadwood piano. Several important composers wrote works for him, including Humprey Searle, Sir Arthur Bliss, and Howard Ferguson.

In the evenings we played 'Whot', or went to the cinema. Brighton in those days was blessed with several cinemas showing the latest French and Italian films. We saw Jacques Tati, Vittorio de Sica, Pagnol, and Totò. In London I saw the original 'Waiting for Godot' at the Arts Theatre.

We had a lot of visitors, including my uncle George and his wife Flo, and my cousin Peter from Australia. David my father never got on very well with his brother: they had very different characters, George being a great extrovert and my father hating any outward show, a basically shy man.

George and Peter came down to Brighton, George taking 16mm film wherever he went. He had by now a very big business in Australia: 'Sunshine Kitchen Cabinets', one of the biggest of its kind in the southern hemisphere he said, based at Sunshine near Melbourne, where he had the prescience to buy a big lot for a factory when he was a young man. The factory burned down, but it was well insured and he built an even bigger factory. The family lived in the smart area of Toorak.

The other friends we saw were the Kingsleys, who brought Lord Rothermere to see us once, as Charles was his financial advisor. Also Marjorie's friends from the theatre, Ivy St. Helier, Eileen Peel, Elizabeth Allen, Beatrice Lillie. Also John Weyman who liked my work and bought several paintings.

We often went to the Theatre Royal, and saw Gielgud in 'Much Ado about Nothing' and later 'King Lear' with sets by Isamu Noguchi. After the impressive performance of Lear, Clive and I went round to Gielgud's dressing room. When the door opened a camp Gielgud greeted us with a bottle of 'champers'- the contrast was unbelievable!

I had a happy life in Hove, in spite of my celibacy (apart from the odd visit to Shepherd's Market) but the exhibition had been something of an anticlimax, and I thought seriously now about exhibiting abroad. It was Italy that attracted me, I felt an affinity with the painting I had seen .

Invitation to my show at the Hanover

In September, then, another trip to Italy, with my mother. We took the Newhaven-Dieppe ferry this time, and stayed at the Lenox Hotel in St. Germain.

The next day I went to Pierre Loeb gallery, but he was away. We had lunch at Benoit, and in the afternoon I went to Jean Helion's house: Joseph had given me an introduction, and I admired his work, from the early abstract paintings to the latest genre pieces. But he also was not at home, and I went again to see him the next day. He was most kind, and showed me the big canvasses he was working on, with a park bench which he had in his remarkable studio.

I showed photographs of my work to various galleries, including the Galerie de France, and the Rive Gauche, but without much success. I went to Nina Dausset gallery and she seemed interested in my work, and gave me an introduction to Victor Brauner whom I went to see in his studio. He liked my work, especially the engravings, and gave me an introduction to the boss of the bookshop La Hune.

The next day the train to Milano. The tourist office gave us the address of a room in a flat as the hotels were booked out. A Signora Ogier in Viale Tunisia had rooms. She was a motherly lady whose husband had been in the paint business, and who had a young son, Claudio. I quickly went to the Brera and saw the Raphael Sposalizio and Piero's Madonna.

The next day I went to the Domus offices to see Signorina Ponti, the daughter of the architect, to whom Joseph had given me an introduction. She gave me the address of Salvatore Fiume near Lake Como. I then went to the Milione gallery and showed my work to Ghiringhelli. He liked it, but suggested the Obelisco in Rome.

We went the next day to see Fiume at Canzo. He had several huge studios for his different activities: painting, sculpture, ceramics, graphics. We had tea in the village with him and his wife, a teacher, and he gave me an introduction to a Milan gallery. The next day I duly went to the house of the gallery owner, Guido Le Noci in 24 Via Petrarca. He liked my work and offered a show in his small gallery 'Apollinaire' in Via Brera, which had only recently opened. This was good news, and gave me encouragement.

On to Padua. I saw the Scrovegni chapel, and Goethe's palm in the Orto Botanico, the to the Venice Biennale with Bacon and Freud in the British pavilion, and Delvaux and Magritte in the Belgian. Also things I had not seen in my previous visit, like the Carpaccios in San Giorgio Schiavoni, and the Museo Correr.

John Weyman was also in Venice at that time, and we had good meals with him at 'La Colomba' and 'Antico Martini'.

We met the painter Santomaso for a drink: my mother liked his work a lot, as well as that of another Venetian painter, de Pisis. Santomaso gave me an introduction to Cardazzo of the Cavallino Gallery, and I showed him my work, which he liked.

After a few days in Venice we took the train back to Milan, where I saw Le Noci again who gave me a book about the painter Meloni. Two days later we took the train to Cannero on Lake Maggiore, and Pallanza, and saw the Villa Taranto which interested me for its Dicksonia tree-ferns and Eucalyptus. I talked to Mr. Cocker the head gardener and learned a lot about the climate and the garden.

The next day my father arrived and we took a rowing-boat out to the castle. From Intra we went to Isola Bella and Isola Madre with its Jubaea spectabilis and Cupressus cashmeriana, a real garden of paradise.

Marjorie & John Weyman at Florians in Venice

We met a Signor Battacchi who was in London at the Savoy, and whose sister-in-law ran the restaurant at Isola Bella. He showed us some villas to let, and one very near the lake at Cannero for sale for £15,000 complete with furniture and a big garden. I saw it many years later and somewhat regretted the fact that my father did not have the courage to buy it. This was not the last time: a year or two later he saw a splendid villa on Cap Ferrat with its own beach for a similar price! This would of course have been a wonderful investment.

Back again to Milan. We stayed at the Palace Hotel, and the next day went to La Scala to see 'The Sleeping Beauty' ballet conducted by Robert Irving, whom we met afterwards, and had lunch with the next day at the Grand Hotel. He was going on to Naples with the company.

My father took the opportunity of visiting a paint company, strangely enough just near the hotel, and I went to the Naviglio Gallery and a big show of Belgian Art at the Permanente with five Magrittes.

In the evening I went to a Rubinstein piano recital at the Teatro Lirico; it was packed and he gave four encores. I felt Milan was very lively and exciting for the arts, and was looking forward to my show at the 'Apollinaire' the next year. I also showed my work to Arturo Schwartz, Duchamp's dealer. He liked my etchings and said he would give me a show of them in November. I also enjoyed the Poldo Pezzoli museum, and the Triennale which was on. We saw Signora Ogier for tea, and ate at Tantalo near the Galleria.

Towards the end of October 1954 we took the night train to Paris, and on to London on the Golden Arrow, my mother confiding her jewellery to a Mr. Ward, a steward on the ferry to get through the customs which were severe in those days. The same evening we took the Brighton Belle: a strange feeling to be back in England after all the activity in Italy.

There was a card from the Hanover, a private view of a Tchelichew show to be opened by Edith Sitwell; a must!

The paintings looked good in the studio and I was eager to start work again. We saw Clive who was about to leave for a concert in Germany, and went to see Hitchcock's 'Rear Window.'

Clive Lythgoe

In London I met Joseph at the Cézanne show at the Tate with his friend Giorgio Bellavitis (splendid name) an architect from Venice, and then to the ICA to hear a talk by Man Ray. There we also met Roland Penrose, Peter Watson and Edward Wright, who was later to become a great friend.

John Weyman gave a cocktail party at his flat, 58 Warwick Square, and Douglas Cooper and John Richardson were also there, and the painter Roy de Maistre who invited me to tea. He had shown at the Hanover, and had carpets by Francis Bacon in his living room.

At Hove I concentrated on my engravings, and also writing articles for a new magazine: 'My Garden'. I wrote pieces on various topics, some under a pseudonym as the editor had plenty of space to fill. I also did a lithograph on the stone at a local printer of a banana. I sold some of these, and met Hans Judah who liked the lithographs. I saw a lot of Joseph in London, and he lent me various books, including Wittkower on Proportion. I also met a Swiss art dealer, Ulrich Gasser, at the ICA. He proposed a possible show in Bern. He had a fascinating portfolio of paintings for sale, including a delightful Bauchant of flowers, and a Magritte. With hindsight I wish I had bought these, and a very big Delvaux

Banana, lithograph

which was for sale for around £200, and is now in Tate Modern: a nude lying on a couch in a classical square. Joseph and I tried to persuade Erika Brausen to give a show of Magritte, but she thought of him as a 'Pompier' painter and not worthy of a show.

We had Christmas in Hove, seeing Clive and some musicians from the Hallé orchestra the next day. The next year, 1955 was to be an important one.

The library at Radnor

In January there was 12° of frost at Radnor, but the palm trees and eucalyptus seemed to be bearing up well, especially the eucalyptus from the snow zone in Victoria: for example E niphophila. The cats were also in good health, that is to say Queenie and Kitty.

I worked hard to get enough paintings ready for the show in Milan. Joseph came down to Brighton to see what I was doing: he liked my painting of Circe, but thought I should pay more attention to perspective. Here began the considerable influence he had on my work. He promised to write a note for the Apollinaire catalogue. In London he was often at the St.George's Gallery bookshop in Cork street, run by his friend Agatha Sadler. My grandfather had had a show of his recent abstract paintings there, when it was run by Basil Jonzen, and now Robert Erskine was exhibiting prints and sold one of mine to the Victoria and Albert Museum.

Joseph and I often used to meet on a Saturday morning and lunch at the Café Torino in Soho, or the Colombina d'Oro. This latter was run by a lady from Grossetto who preferred to speak Italian, and gave the menu in English only under protest. She would stand in the centre of the restaurant and tell us what the weather was like in Grosseto, or read from her local newspaper. Her husband was confined to the kitchen downstairs.

As usual I made my own Christmas cards, and we saw Clive, Peter and Derrick Grainger from the Financial Times, as well as Clive's parents.

I left for Milan in early March 1955, and took the night train from Paris. By chance I met my school friend Eustace Gibbs, now a diplomat, at the station, and we had breakfast together.

I went to see Le Noci at the gallery and got some catalogues with Joseph's article, which Le Noci did not entirely agree with, as he could not see my work as having a connection with the industrial society. After they had been released by the Sovrintendenza I helped unpack the paintings, and Le Noci was pleased with them, as was Fabio Mauri who was having the show there at the moment. I exchanged a print for a drawing with Mauri: I liked this practice in Italy, there was much exchange, also of ideas, between artists,unlike the dreary art school atmosphere of England.

Le Noci was most kind: he invited me to lunch at his house most days, and his wife was an excellent cook. I managed to contact Joseph's friend Pat Crooke, the architect, and we had dinner and went to see Visconti's film 'Senso', which Fiume later said had no *senso!*

I telephoned people that Erika had given me introductions to, including Marino Marini. I spoke to his wife, and she said she would come the next day, also Cardazzo turned up and the lady from the Del Sole gallery.I did an interview on RAI radio, and the Signorina who lived below Signora Ogier bought a painting, a satirical work of two politicians. Also Meloni and Fornasetti came in to the tiny gallery, and Carlo Pagano the architect.

It was a very exciting time for me, I had not met with any such enthusiasm and knowledge of modern art in England.

In front of my paintings at the Apollinaire Gallery, Milan

I had lunch at the Ristorante Bagutta, and Lollobrigida was eating spaghetti at the next table: I was fascinated to see how she sucked up the pasta. I also met an American music student, a baritone, who told me of an interesting bordello, I think in Corso Magenta. I went along. It was astonishing: a bare room with benches along the sides, and a sort of pulpit for the Madame. There were thirty or so, mostly young, men seated on the benches and three or four ladies past their prime in mini-skirts and feathers parading up and down. Every now and then a man would get up and take one of the women up a staircase which led off the room. Some minutes later he would come down again, pay and leave. What struck me was how open and overtly carnal the operation was. I did not really feel like having a go.

I went, at Fiume's invitation, to see Respighi's 'La Fiamma' at La Scala: he had done the sets. In the interval I was allowed on the stage, and met Respighi's widow, my idea of how a distinguished Italian widow should be: tragic and sad.

Schwartz offered to do a book of my work for lire 60,000; I do not know why I did not take him up on it. I met Music and went to see his show at the Naviglio. I met Piero Dorazio and his wife, he was having the show after mine.

A few days later I left on a sort of mini Grand Tour of Italy: first to Bologna.I stayed at Hotel Moderno, and visited San Petronius and the PInacoteca. The next day to Ferrara. I took the bus, I saw the Cossa painting at Palazzo Schifanoia, and looked at the Garofalo ceiling in the Museo Spina, and the Palazzo Diamante which Joseph had talked about, and the remnants of Alberti at the cathedral.

Via Bologna again, I left for Florence and stayed at the Fenice, via Martelli. I did the usual tourist rounds and ate at the Giglio Rosso. and after a day there I took a train to Arezzo, staying at the Continentale. I was overcome by the Piero murals and finished the day with Totò in 'Oro di Napoli'. The next day on by bus to Borgo San Sepolcro. In those days it was a small unspoilt town surrounded by a wall. I saw the magnificent Piero della Francesca resurrection, and the curator of the museum took me on his bicycle to see a newly discovered 'Head of an Angel' in the local hall where the band practised. Some workmen were removing plaster from a wall, and discovered just this part of the fresco that had been painted there. It was an extraordinary moment to have a sort of preview of this beautiful painting.

Piero della Francesca, Head

Later that day I took the bus to Urbino, where I stayed at the Albergo Italia, where it seemd from the visitors' book that every other English person had stayed. After dinner I had a look at the Palazzo Ducale, and the next day went inside to see the Piero 'Flagellation' which I had heard all about from Fiume, but also the 'Mystery of the Host' by Uccello. There was something marvellous about Laurana's building, a type of architecture that I had not seen before.

I also walked up to Raphael's birthplace, and talked to the old lady who looked after the rather modest house. She told me that her great dream was to go to Domodossola and watch the express train with its windows lit up at night, on its way to Switzerland.

The same day I paid the hotel and took the bus to Fano, and the train to Rome, a tiring journey mostly along the coast. I stayed at the Hotel Inghilterra, the first of several times, a hang-out of English writers and artists. In fact the novelist Elizabeth Bowen was staying there, and I talked to her at dinner, as well as to the Scottish baritone Ian Wallace who was singing in a marvellous performance of Rossini's 'La Cenerentola' which I went to see at the Teatro Nazionale.

Two American friends of Elizabeth Bowen proposed a trip around Rome in their car, and we went to Tivoli, to the Villa d'Este with its incredible water-works and fountains, also the Protestant cemetery and Monte Testaccio built with broken potsherds.

I was sitting one morning on the Pincio when a doctor sat on the bench beside me, and we started talking about the beautiful Roman women passing by. He told me of a *casa chiusa* or brothel in Via Avignonesi, near the Piazza Barberini, and said there were some lovely girls. Of course my curiosity got the better of me, and after some difficulty finding the right building. I was ushered into a small *salone* by an elderly lady, quite well dressed, who asked me what was my pleasure. She left and three or four very attractive girls came in, and I chose two and we went upstairs. The house was very well regulated with medical checks and and a lot of washing, and I had a good time! I learnt later that the lady's name was Signor Trabucchi and that the building had later been used as a set by Roberto Rossellini, and was now a hotel.

I showed my work to one or two galleries, and saw Derek Hill at the British School. I went to the Vatican, and to San Pietro in Montorio to see the little *tempietto* of Bramante, exquisite. I went to the Schneider Gallery, an American who said he would give me a show the next spring.

The next day I took the train to Orvieto and the Signorellis which I admired a lot, and then an afternoon train to Siena.

I enjoyed the Siennese primitives in the Pinacoteca, especially the curious compositions of Lorenzetti: the little boat on the shore. I also liked the freshness of the Pintoricchios in the cathedral; amazing colour. Siena had a strange atmosphere for me. The next day I took the train to Milan, changing at Empoli and Florence, and arriving in the afternoon. I went straight to Signora Ogier's flat, and fortunately she could put me up.

I went to see Le Noci at the gallery and met Pino Serpi who was now showing there. Le Noci helped me fill in a form in quintuplicate for the customs to send home my unsold paintings: that is one advantage of the European Union today, a little less bureaucracy! I talked to Fiume who said he would like to come to England, which desire was realised a year or two later. I had a letter from Gasser who was in Zurich, so decided to stop off there on my way home.

I saw a magnificent Bonnard show at the Permanente, and went round the galleries. I bought an Italian flag at Rinascente, and a box of chocolates for Signora Ogier and her son Claudio. In the evening I went to see Meneghini-Callas (sic) at the Scala in Rossini's 'Il Turco in Italia'. It was delightful, especially the bear in a Neapolitan hat.

I left for Zurich, and had the address of Anna Intermeyer where Gasser was staying. She was something of a popular figure in Zurich; the owner of the 'Nord-Sud' cinema which showed French films, and the nearby Café Select. She lived on Seefeltstrasse, and was also a painter. Gasser introduced me to some Zurich galleries, including Chicchio Haller and Palette, also a lithography studio. We had lunch with the sculptor Stanzani and his wife, and the next day Anna took us on a tour to Lake Constance where we visited a primitive painter (and rabbit breeder), Adolf Dietrich. Gasser had arranged a show for him at Arthur Jeffress Gallery in June of that year. He had many paintings turned to the wall and when Gasser asked about prices he was surprised how astute the old man was: he was no primitive when it came to business. We went on to the Schloss Arenenberg where Napleon's sister had lived and died. Back to Zurich where Anna made a delicious rhubarb soufflé.

'Babo' by Adolf Dietrich

I had a long talk with Ulrich Gasser: he could see how much I had enjoyed life in Italy and asked me why I was returning to England. I could only reply that it was to work and see my parents, but I realised that this was in a way a cowardly attitude. Comfort first! I took the train straight through to London.

6

LOVE and LONDON

It was strange to be back in England and working again. Life seemed dull and slow and I realised I had little in common with my contemporary English painters. I went to the Music show at Arthur Jeffress. I met David Carritt, Lucien Freud, and Saffi from the Italian Institute, as well as talking to Zoran Music. I saw Dali on the television talking about the Young Contemporaries exhibiton, he said the work was very 'dirrrty,' meaning the colours of the paintings! I also remember, around that time, seeing Cocteau interviewed and trying to seduce the male interviewer.

I was beginning to do much more architectural, or geometrical subjects. I did a painting with a Greek priest and opening cupboards in a landscape, later sold to John Weyman. He had now bought several of my paintings. Ulrich Gasser and Anna Intermeyer from Zurich came down to Radnor, and saw my new work, which they liked. In July I began to design some costumes and sets for opera, perhaps inspired by a visit to Glyndebourne to see Sena Jurinac in 'Don Giovanni', also 'The Rake's Progress'.

At the beginning of August I met a mother and daughter at Clive's place: Cardie Duxbury and her daughter Ann Bickford-Smith. Ann was a textile designer and painter and lived with her mother in Brighton. They had come from South Africa, but Ane's father was from a Cornish family. They were friends with John Cranko the ballet choreographer from South Africa, and he was coming down from London to visit them. They asked me along, and I later went to Cranko's house in Pimlico to show him my designs which he liked, but nothing came of it.

I soon became very fond of Ann, and began to see a lot of her and her very possessive mother Cardie, who laid down the law as far as Ann's life went, and I felt sorry for her. I could see that she needed to get away, and later that year I helped her to do it.

Ann, myself, and Gunnera at Radnor

I visited Ann and Cardie often, and met several interesting friends of theirs, including the explorer Nicholas Guppy and the architect Joseph Emberton, who had designed Simpson's shop in Piccadilly, with an interior by Moholy Nagy. I showed him my work, and he suggested I laid out my paintings in an architectural way, with a ground plan, and constructing from that. This interested me as I was fascinated by perspective and had just bought Abbott's book on the subject.

I had now decided to try to find a studio in London. I could see my life was changing, and that I had already left it late to leave the comfort and easiness of living with my parents. I went to various estate agents in London, and saw a really splendid studio in Glebe Place, Chelsea, but I could not make my mind up about it. And then Ruck and Ruck the estate agents told me of a studio to let in Thurloe Square, South Kensington. It belonged to a Lady Stott, a miniature painter who nevertheless was willing to leave her huge easel. It was a real painter's studio in a curious building on the south side of the square, and shaped like a slice of cheese. I took a liking to it, and after my parents had a look, I signed the lease. This was a very exciting move for me, and I brought my paintings from Brighton, and bought some new furniture.

It was one large room with a big north window, and small bathroom and kitchenette. On another floor the painter Matthew Smith had had his studio and there was a photographer above and a jeweller beneath. The tenant had the right of a key to the splendid gardens in the square, and there was a caretaker who would do cleaning. I was delighted with it, and bought a sofa bed that could be folded during the day.

At the same time my parents were looking for a furnished flat for the winter, and found one in the King's Road, on the corner of Bramerton Street. It was in the same building as the famous Lesbian club, the Gateways, and belonged to a Mr. Salmon, a philosopher. He was a bird lover, and many small birds were allowed to fly freely in the living-room, which certainly would have put off many tenants, but not my mother with her love of animals.

We had however a mishap: there was a kerosene stove to heat the living-room, and one weekend they left it on by mistake, and it burnt out with black smoke coating the room, including the birds, who had to be washed one by one. Not all survived.

I did a lot of work painting the studio at 5 Thurloe Square, with Ann helping me. I painted decorations over the doorways, and managed to cook in the tiny kitchen. One of the few drawbacks to the studio was the noise of the underground which ran nearby from Sloane Square towards South Kensington station. In time I became used to the vibrations.

I fell in love with Ann, and she with me. She came to live nearby in London, much to her mother's anger, and my mother's incomprehension. I have many of her letters, tender and affectionate, and I found her a job with Robert Erskine at St. George's Gallery in Cork Street. We used to have picnics in nearby Green Park, and see my parents in the King's Road.

After a while I could not cope with these strong emotions. I had a near nervous breakdown, and went to see a psychiatrist recommended by Joseph Rykwert in Gloucester Place, whom he called 'uncle,' Dr. Elkisch. He was a Jungian and I had to write down my dreams which were often of Italy. He said to me "Is it true you hate *all* the English?" He later came around to my studio and was quite surprised at the quality of my work.

I was still going down to Radnor at the weekends and saying hello to my cat, Kitty, and to Brighton to see Clive, who was now also moving to London. He had a new partner, François Giuliani who was from Alger, and later would go with Clive to New York.

Cardie, Ann's mother, was very resentful of her daughter coming to London and staged some hysterical illnesses to recapture Ann's attention. I found these scenes very disturbing. A year later Ann and I were still together, but then she went on a trip to Capri invited by her friends Anne and Vittorio Gargiulo, a Caprese teacher and his English wife who had a sports clothes boutique on the island. Ann's letters were becoming more and more distant, and she was meeting interesting people like John Gielgud, and a Prince Parente from Naples, who had a son by the daughter of the Duke of Portland.

It soon turned out that Ann was having an affair with Parente, and distressed I went to Capri after her, to no avail. I later met her in Rome on my way back, but I could see the affair was ending. It was sad for me, and looking back I can see how much it was my lack of experience, especially sexual. My friends Joseph Rykwert and Edward Wright were of great help to me in my mental anguish.

In 1957 Salvatore Fiume came to London as the scene designer for Aida at Covent Garden. I introduced him to David

Decoration in my studio

Webster, and showed him around London. He remarked that as there were no people in the streets, the houses were the people with their windows for eyes, door for mouth, and chimneys for ears. He had arrived with his secretary whom he was trying to seduce on the night train from Milan without success. Later in his life he had great success as a 'donnaiolo' or ladykiller. But it seemed he was no match for the choreographer of the opera, Margherita Wallmann, who insisted on moving his papier-mâché boulders around on the stage to his fury. I went back stage to see him painting directly on the costumes, and then later to the premier. He came down to Radnor, and also to my studio. I was now painted quite rigid geometrical subjects and this annoyed him. He asked me "Did God tell you which colours to use?" To some extent I took this to heart, but he later wrote to me excusing his intemperate remarks. But John Weyman also, who had bought a number of my paintings, lamented what he saw as a loss of sensuality from my earlier work.

Joseph was not enamoured of Fiume and what he saw as his pretensions (which he attributed himself to his fiery Sicilian upbringing.)

Every Saturday Edward Wright and his wife Kitty had an open house for artists and friends where they lived at Swiss Cottage. Edward had designed the catalogue for the exhibition in 1956 at the Whitechapel Gallery 'This is Tomorrow', and Reyner Banham, Theo Crosby, Monica Pigeon and Richard Hamilton were often around. With Monica Pigeon I designed a memorial for a South American country, but the dictator was deposed and the project came to nothing. I also helped Joseph making his maquette at the last minute for the Liverpool Cathedral project.

Also in 1956 Joseph, Edward and I went to Marseilles for an exhibition on the roof of Corbusier's 'Unité d'Habitation', an immense block of flats on the outskirts of the city. It held one of the first cybernetic ballets of Nicholas Schöffer, also Maurice Béjart, Soto, and others. I met Soto again in Paris where he was playing the guitar in a club to earn a living for his family. Another excursion with Joseph was the Brussels World Fair a year or two later. Overleaf myself in front of the British Pavilion.

Back at Radnor, where I retreated most weekends, my father had decided to sell William Harland and son. As a paint manufacturer it was having problems: new methods of production were becoming available, sidelining the crafts of varnish making and

Joseph Rykwert and my painting

Myself at Brussels World Fair, 1957

colour mixing which had been the pride of the old generation of employees. He sold to an American printing ink company, Ault and Wyborg from Cincinnati. My only interest in the company was the poster they had commissioned from Toulous Lautrec. However they made the best offer my father could find for the company, and he sold it receiving also shares in the parent company, and a seat on the British board, chaired by a Mr. Kennedy.

Erika Brausen promised to come to see my new work if I picked her up in Bolton Gardens where she lived. I did so, but she was not very enthusiastic about my new work. At present I had no plans for new exhibitions, but made many friends in London, some coming from the Royal College nearby to see my work. Edouardo Paolozzi for example, and Robin Denny and Anthony Hill.

In 1957 my grandfather died in Torquay. He and my grandmother had visited Radnor, and I could see that he was thin and unwell. He had cancer and was in a clinic. He had had a big exhibition at Plymouth Museum, and had lately been painting abstract gouaches. When I went to see him he had some fruit by his bed, and said to me "I'm thinking of painting that when I get up." But he never got up. I was alone in the room with him when he died, and when he saw the tears in my eyes, he smiled and said "Chin up!"

He was buried in Plymouth, in a cemetery that was later to be built over, and his remains transferred elsewhere. He was a good man, and if not a great artist, he inspired many of his young students when he taught and retained a poetical view of life. He told a story of being in the officers' mess in the Airforce (he was in fact one of the first two men to wear Airforce uniform when it was developed from the Royal Naval Air Service) and seeing through the window a white horse in the twilight, he enthusiastically pointed out this vision to the other officers. But the aesthetic aspect passed them by, and they just said "It's a horse, so what?" But my grandfather would write a poem about it. Later on he was furious with the City Council in Torquay for spending money on fairy lights along the front, instead of possible Arts Council exhibitions. In today's climate when the arts are so well sponsored and diffused his attitude and anger are difficult to comprehend, but at the time the frustration was all too real, and he did what he could to improve matters in terms of the understanding of the arts.

I was now working on some new ideas, one of which was the placing of objects on an existing painting, that is to say painted objects which cast shadows on the original painting. The reverse of this was cutting holes in a painting (figuratively) to see what was underneath - in fact another painting. I have now published a book 'Magic of the Picture Plane' Lulu, 2006, which explains as far as is possible this practice. It resulted in some ambiguous images largely generated by linear perspective. In some cases I would lay out shadows, and then construct the objects that cast them, so that the shadow became as much part of the subject as the object itself.

I also invented, in my new studio, a system of conceptual works which must have been among the first of their kind. I set up an easel with a blackboard, and supposed that virtual images were passing over the board and could be trapped by a drawing or painting. Of course this flux of images was totally imaginary, but gave the representations an ephemeral quality as they passed from north to south, or east to west, as it were.

For these paintings I would prepare a cartoon on cover paper, and transfer this to the canvas with carbon paper. It was quite a laborious process but was the only way I succeeded in achieving the desired result. Colour also was important, but especially for delineating layers, a sort of coding. But I wanted to produce also a mysterious and attractive image.

I also at that point became interested in photography, and bought an Exacta reflex camera, and enlarger. I hoped to construct more subjects in cardboard, photograph them, and then transfer to canvas, but this happened a good deal later.

I still had not lost my love of Italy, and went one summer to paint at the Misses Lewis's school in Positano. Edna Lewis had set up the school in 1952, and I thought it was a way of

Ribbons and shelves, 1957

doing some work in the sun, though in fact it only resulted in one small painting. But it had another result: meeting Annalita.

Annalita Marsigli was a student at Barnard College in New York, having previously been educated at Vassar. She was on holiday with her mother, the Marchesa Maria Luisa, or Marlys, and they were staying at the Palazzo Murat in Positano. They dropped in at the art school, and after chstting we had dinner together at a trattoria near the sea.

Annalita (short for Anna Ippolita) was not especially interested in painting, but we talked about literature, and I learned about her illustrious family from Bologna who had entertained Galileo, and Brecht had been to visit to find out more for his play. They also had a connection with Alberti, though not of course in the direct line, and an ancestor had taught at Bologna University. This was the famous Ippolita who taught anatomy behind a curtain, as she was so beautiful the students otherwise might have been put off their studies.

Annalita and her mother told me they were going on to Capri where they had an aunt and a cousin staying. They asked if I was coming along to Capri, and nothing loath I booked a room at the Hotel Residenza. I was a little uneasy at the thought of meeting Ann, and in fact I believe I caught sight of her in one of the alleyways. But I congratulated myself that I was over my love and attraction.

After some days at the 'Canzone del Mare', Gracie Fields' club, and the beach, and walks to Malaparte's villa, Marlys suggested that I drive around Italy with them in their new Mercedes. I explained that I did not drive, but Marlys thought that anyway it would be good to have a man in the car.

We first drove up to Rome where I met Annalita's father, the Marchese Giovanni. He was a small busy man, very emotional and direct, and he had an Alfa Romeo. We were to meet later on in Bologna.

Our journey took us up to Lago Bolsena, where Annalita had a cousin, Prince Giovanni del Drago. He owned the immense castle on the lake, and to make ends meet he had opened it as a hotel, and restaurant.

He was studying architecture in the States, and restoring the castle. He also owned an island on the lake which he took us to by boat,

Annalita and myself in Capri (the aunt behind)

and it boasted several chapels decorated by Benozzo Gozzoli, a real little paradise. We also stopped in Perugia, where an admirer of Annalita was waiting, Assisi, Spoleto and on to Marlys's family home, somewhere near Imola.

The Marsigli palace was in the centre of Bologna, in Via d'Azeglio, and I met Annalita's grandmother, a formidable old lady who had become quite a very well known personality in Bologna.She dressed in black, and was famous for her black hats and her musical recitals in the grand ballroom of the palazzo. Her soloists included musicians like Arthur Rubinstein and Roberto Murolo (until he was involved in a sex sxandal!)

Annalita was flying back to New York with her mother, and I was sad not to be seeing her. She suggested that I come to New York and see what it was like, and after much thought I decided to go on the Queen Mary in the autumn of 1959. The journey took about four days, and I enjoyed the new experience. One of the other travellers was the brother of the actress Angela Lansbury who was already famous in Hollywood. I took a few small paintings with me and hoped to show them to galleries, and also paint some portraits.

Annalita found me a room in a friend's apartment on the East River and I bought a cheap easel and painted in my bedroom. But it was Annalita's mother that I saw the most of, as Annalita was studying at Barnard College and had a busy life. Whereas Marlys had a very social life going to charity events and was happy to have me along, as her husband the Marchese would rather eat his dinner in front of the television. They lived in a big Park Avenue apartment, in fact the same block as Marlene Dietrich. Salvador Dalì was a friend of Annalita's, and came to a small exhibition I made in their apartment and showed me another side of the eccentric showman that he was. He liked my work and we talked about Italy and the painters he admired. He told me to go one day to see Canova's studio at Possagno near Venice, which I later did and enjoyed. He always stayed at the St Regis hotel, and I went to several of his exhibition openings and events. He was of course a great self-publicist and I saw a very different person from the one I had chatted to about art.

Another friend of Dalì's was a painter from Paris, now living in New York, Mimi Fogt. She gave a dinner for Dalì and Duchamp, whose portrait she had painted, and told me afterwards that Dalì scarcely dared open his

Annalita with my portrait of her

Cast of 'Le Donne Curiose' at Columbia University. I am back row right, and Dolph Sweet on my left. Camilla Trinchieri is seated in front of me.

mouth, he was so much in awe of the intellectual Duchamp.

Mimi and I used to go to gallery openings on Saturday evening and savour the pretentious atmosphere of many of them. Mimi went to live with her husband in Mexico City, and I lost touch with her until forty years later when she was living in Portugal. Sadly she died soon after I had begun a correspondence with her.

I often took the bus up to Barnard College which was near Columbia University, and have lunch with the Italian women who were friends of Annalita. Camilla Trinchieri, Fiammetta Farace, and Bimba Tucci. They commented on their feelings about New York, determined to preserve their Italian sensibilities.

Signora Bovè, head of the Italian department, put on a performance of 'Le Donne Curiose' of Goldoni, and asked me to do the (very simple) decor for the stage at the Casa Italiana at Columbia. Then, short of an actor, she asked me if I would like the part of Florindo, the young lover of Rosaura who was played by Camilla Trinchieri. I hesitated as I doubted if my Italian was up to the mark, but finally agreed, doing some voice lab practice beforehand.

Our producer was Dolph Sweet, the head of Drama at Barnard, and a method actor who wanted the Italians in the cast to think twice before uttering a word. This of course did not work, and on the first night they came upstage and acted in the Italian fashion. Poor Sweet was furious, but there was nothing to be done!

I have to say that, in spite of my ineptitude in Italian, I thoroughly enjoyed these few days of acting, and it is with regret that I did not pursue it further, even if not as a career.

I made many friends in New York, not having expected to like the city, being full of English prejudices about America. One thing I was not prepared for was the snobbishness I found: where you lived, whom you saw, where you ate. I suppose this is the same in any big city, but I did not expect it in New York.

While Annalita's father, a doctor, worked in forensic medicine, the Marchesa his wife turned up her nose when I said I was meeting an Italian artist in the village. Certain areas of the city were taboo for her. I painted a portrait of her with a fan and ball gown, and a rope of pearls, which I think pleased her, but which I think her husband and daughter found slightly ridiculous.

Annalita had a number of admirers, rich young men, whom she played with to some extent, a wily Italian girl. I gave her an engagement ring, but I do not think I was what Marlys had in mind for her, and a romance eventually came to nothing. We had an interest in literature in common, but apart from a trip to Jamaica with her, I did not see that much of her. However I am grateful to her for having introduced me to American life. It was worth the six months I spent there, so much so that at the end of that time I seriously thought about staying and not returning to England.

Annalita knew an Englishman called Nigel Mathieson who had a flat on East 74th Street, and was looking for a lodger. We got on well, and I moved there from the East River apartment, and paid for my stay with a portrait of Nigel. The only drawback for me was that I slept on a couch in the living-room, and he had parties of young jet setters there until late every night.

Nigel was a Harrovian and his English accent, like mine, seemed spell-binding to the Americans. He more or less lived on his Englishness, invited out, as I was, to soirees given by blue rinse ladies who seemed to rule the roost in New York. I met my old school friend James Coats who was now dealing in Pre-Raphaelite paintings and living in a hotel, and he introduced me to a certain Phoebe, the owner of 'Phoebe's Whamburger' on Madison Avenue. I went to see her, and she offered me

Myself as Florindo

a trip to Bermuda as a bouncer in the evenings, and a place to paint during the day. She appeared in a negligé and appeared to me intent on seduction on a slow boat to Bermuda. Everything considered, being a bouncer was not my forte, and I turned down the invitation.

At the weekends the Marsigli family would take off in the car to visit stately homes or go skiing in New York State. This was the only time in my life I have been skiing, and was not greatly enamoured of the experience. Another excursion was a trip to Jamaica with Annalita, where I met Leslie Murray-Aynsley, my parents' friend who worked there for the British Council, and with whom I had exchanged my piano. We took a train ride across the island, and stayed at Port Antonio. What I remember most was the botanical garden with its blue Jacaranda flowers covering the lawns. There were some delightful beaches we visited, and the food was good. But my relationship with Annalita did not really improve.

Through Marlys I met some extraordinary people in New York. For example Princess Eristavi who lived on Fifth Avenue with mechanical toys moving around her apartment, and a chauffeur who drove her car round and around the block until she called down for him, as there was no parking space. She had six stalls permanently booked at the Lincoln Center and called me one morning to ask me if I would like to go to Parsifal that evening and take some friends. I picked up the tickets and rang friends like Mimi, but nobody was available and I ended up sitting in the best seats in the house, empty seats on both sides of me. Then there was Mrs. Woolyheart who was supposed to be an art lover and took me out to dinner, I think at the Russian tearooms. But she did not buy anything. A couple who did however buy my work were the Harold Johnsons who lived in Southampton, Long Island, and bought some big paintings of mine when they later came to London and stayed at Claridges.

Annalita was a great friend of Gordon Wasson, a banker who was also an amateur botanist and did much research into the Mexican 'Magic Mushroom'. Annalita had some pills of a synthesised version of this drug, and came round to where I was staying one evening. She asked my weight and gave me some tablets to swallow. The effect was not instantaneous and she went home thinking it had not worked. However after an hour or so I had strange hallucinations of floating down a Chinese river, and did some work on a portrait: an eye, which looked marvellous. The bell rang, and it was Marlys asking me out to one of her soirees. When she saw me she assumed I was drunk, and quickly left. The next day when the drug had worn off I looked at my work, and it did not seem marvellous at all.

After six months of New York I was beginning to feel homesick, and missing Radnor and London. My 'engagement' with Annalita was not bearing fruit: I had given her a sapphire ring which I had bought in London at Christies, but although there was great affection between us, her mother was not in favour of my marriage, and even even suggested the other Italian girls at Barnard as possible girlfriends. I took back the ring, and decided to leave for London.

Two memories: a meeting of the Poetry Society of America, of which Annalita was the youngest member as her mother boasted. Robert Graves received the Society's gold medal, in front of poets like Marianne Moore and Ogden Nash. He looked at it quizzically, then bit it to see if it really was gold. There was a deathly silence in the room.

The other memory was the first night of 'Arlecchino, Servitore di Due Padroni' by the Piccolo Teatro of Milano. Dalì and Gala were in the front row, Gala looking snake-like as ever. Afterwards a party to meet the actors, including Ferruccio Soleri. Oh, and my first meeting with Italo Calvino at the Premio Prezzolini..

This time I left on the Rotterdam with many regrets, but also homesickness, back to Southampton. But it was not the last time I saw Annalita.

David Russell 'Three girls in a garden' Casein on paper (Annalita in the centre)

7

BACK to EUROPE and ITALY

My grandfather's death meant that my grandmother was alone in Torquay, and although she was a strong and independent person my mother brought her up to Radnor. This did not please my father enormously, and he was very sarcastic about her.

By now we had a new couple at Radnor, the Lloyds, Gordon and Rose, as gardener-chauffeur and cook-housekeeper. They lived in the cottage attached to the stables. My parents gave up the flat in Brighton, and bought the lease of a house in Thurloe Square, on the same side as my studio. I was not very pleased about this, but said nothing. I could persuade myself that it would be convenient to pop in for a meal from time to time. They rented the basement to students.

I could not leave Italy for long, and after staying a while in Fiesole I rented a top floor flat in Florence, in Piazza San Giovanni, with a roof terrace overlooking the Duomo and Baptistery. I began to make many friends there, including a friend of the Marsiglis, Baronessa Livia Scaglione. She was from Trieste and had an extremely elegant penthouse apartment overlooking the Arno near the Ponte Vecchio. She introduced me to the local society at her soirees and dinners. She also had contacts with a gallery near the Piazza Signoria, Spinetti, and I arranged to have an exhibition there.

This was in 1961, and Annalita brought her grandmother from Bologna to see the show. She insisted in going to Doney in Via Tornabuoni for lunch, in a horse carriage taxi. My parents also came to Florence to see the show, and I took them to meet Annalita in Bologna. My father liked the small flat I had rented, and offered to buy it, but I was not at all sure at the time that I wanted to stay longer in Florence. My parents went on to Ischia where my father had mud treatment for the arthritis that he was beginning to suffer from in his shoulders.

catalogue cover of Spinetti show.

The Spinetti show was quite successful and I sold two paintings to Livia Scaglione as well as a number of others to Florentine collectors, including the painting illustrated here to Giuliano Prezzolini, the son of the famous journalist. A few of the paintings were purely geometrical, a series that I was to continue when I returned to London.

However I was enjoying my life in Florence, and made some great friends including the painter Donald Sutphin and his wife Caroline, and Pino Manos a Sardinian painter and architect and his girlfriend Carole who later went to live in London. As I have said I also met many Florentines at Livia Scaglione's apartment, and they invited this unattached bachelor in turn.

I also met the English painter Tony Morgan who was in love with a French woman called Geneviève, and showed me her letters. He was living at the time in the Torre of Bellosguardo, and doing dark paintings. Back in England they invited me to their wedding at Hampton Court. They were later to come and live in Florence in a studio and flat belonging to Daniel Milhaud, another painter. They remained great friends.

After renting the flat in Florence I took off for Venice for several months, renting an artist's studio in the Dorso Duro near the Ponte dei Pugni and opposite the Carmine. It had a small mezzanine for sleeping, and kitchenette, and was right on the canal. I heard the soothing sound of lapping water when the boats passed by, and ate at the trattoria most days on the opposite *riva*, doing the Telegraph crossword while eating.

In Venice I met several English expatriates including the doyenne of the English colony, Christina Thoresby.

Christina played the organ in the English church, and taught Armenian students on San Lazzaro, meeting with an accident there one time when a student pulled out a knife on her. One of her main passions was her cats of which she had several. I remember one of them had to be put down, and she slipped his coffin with a weight into the canal. A day or two later we were walking near the Fenice and she went pale looking over the side of a bridge: the box with her cat was floating by. Later on she went to live just opposite Da Manin and I often had a drink or meal with her in their splendid garden.

In a way I loved Venice more than Florence, and often set off walking and exploring the city, always ending up somewhere familiar. I now enjoy the novels of Donna Leon which take me back nostalgically to Venice.

Peggy Guggenheim often came to eat near my studio with her dogs, and I had dinner in her palazzo once. I cannot say I took to her very much, but I knew her daughter Pegeen and Ralph Romney in London. I quarrelled once with Romney at the ICA, but I no longer remember the argument!

I also met the de Robilands, where Christina had lived before moving. in the Ca' Mocenigo where Byron had stayed with his menagerie. They invited me to see the Regatta from their balcony, and I talked to Prince Alexander of Yugoslavia who told me about his experiences at Gordonstoun and how unhappy Prince Charles was at the school.

Annalita's sister Isabella had married the son of a newspaper proprietor, Paolazzi. who had a splendid Venetian Villa at Martellago, near Venice. I went to stay a night or two there with Annalita and her mother, and I remember a lunch in the park behind the house with the local parish priest and a mynah bird who flew through the trees whistling the Italian national anthem. The villa had a wing which housed a theatre supposedly used by Goldoni. I believe it is now a golf club. Marlys persuaded me to buy a set of china gnomes as a present for the Paolazzis.

I painted several pictures in Venice, inspired by the light and colours. I also took in all the paintings in the churches and museums, and also Goldoni's plays when there was one in the theatre. I especially admired Cesco Baseggio in 'Sior Todero Brontolon' and 'Le Baruffe Chiozzotte.' The harmonies of the Venetian dialect, however, were only to be spoken by Venetian actors in my view, to see a Florentine actress playing Goldoni, did not function at all for me. A friend of mine, Alex Gross, later translated 'La Guerra' into English.

Another encounter in Florence was with an American student, David Block, who later moved to London and became a great friend. There was also Carla Guiscardi who had a small flat in Via Banche Nuove, near the Rucellai palazzo. She was kind to me when I no longer had the flat in Piazza San Giovanni, and put me up in spite of the very modest conditions of her place: no bathroom and no refrigerator for example.

She had fallen on hard times, in spite of having been married to a rich Count with a big Villa on the way to Fiesole, the Villa Camerata. However he had divorced her, and died, and she was now searching through archives to get government compensation.

Annalita at the Ca' della Nave, Martellago

It was at Carla's that I met an Australian, Guy Petherbridge, who was on his way to London to study paper restoration at Goldsmiths College. He pronounced 'Guy' in the French fashion as he had had a French girlfriend. He had been in Greece and had bought a house on the then very primitive island of Sikinos in the Cyclades.

Another great friend I encountered around the same time in Florence was John Phillips, an American who rented a small flat in the palazzo of Francesco Guicciardini, a friend of his. I had seen him around Florence eating alone in restaurants with his grey poodle Orlando, and had wondered who he was, supposing he was Italian. I cannot remember where we met, though probably at a party, and found that he was also a great friend of the writer Violet Trefusis who lived in the fabulous Villa l'Ombrellino at Bellosguardo, looking over Florence.

On roof terrace, Piazza San Giovanni

When I was having my show at Spinetti I took my parents to meet Violet, and John became a great companion of my mother many years later. Violet was certainly a 'Grande Dame' with a very authoritative manner, but at the same time a feminine sophistication perhaps due to her years of Parisian social life and her wide circle of friends in the Arts.

When I first met Violet I had long hair, as was the fashion then, and she said to me "Mr. Russell, are you a Beatle?" Once, not long before she died, I had dinner at l'Ombrellino, and her maid had brought down a lobster from her flat in rue Cherche-Midi in Paris. She did not eat much after getting her butler to find a nutcracker for the claws, but I was very sick that night: I think the lobster had been too long in the car.

Marjorie, John and Orlando

One of Violet's great friends was Winnaretta Singer, the wife of Prince Polignac, and another friend of Winnaretta was another friend of mine in Florence: the painter Anna Scotti.

Anna lived in Via Romana in Florence, but also had a small house right on the sea at Tellaro in Liguria. I exchanged my studio in London for her house, and fell asleep at night to the sound of the waves lapping against the wall of the house. While staying in Tellaro I met an

83

Englishman staying at the local hotel with his wife. He suggested a game of chess after dinner, and we played on the hotel terrace. He won quite easily, unsurprisingly as it turned out, as he was the British Chess Champion, H.O'D. Alexander. He also played a mean game of scrabble.

Back in London I had quite a social life in the mid-sixties. Annalita gave me an introduction to Bruce Winston, the son of Harry Winston, the 'Napoleon of the Diamond Trade.' Bruce had his twenty-first birthday party at the Hungry Horse restaurant in the Fulham Road, and we did some clubbing, dating two Welsh girls. Bruce had met Annabel King, tne English daughter of a General in the Army. I was with Bruce in a pub in Knightsbridge and he told me to go to Harrods and pick up his girlfriend and bring her to the pub. I asked him how I would recognise her, and he said she was a ballerina, and walked with her toes pointed outwards. It was Christmas time and she was doing part-time work in the Harrods confectionery department. I waited at the entrance, and spotted her precisely because of her walk.

Bruce and Annabel got married and had a reception at Claridges, and I took photographs of the wedding. Bruce went on a sort of diamond apprenticeship in Antwerp, but he was never really integrated into the business like his brother Ronnie. When he went back to New York his father only gave him a menial job opening doors.

Guy Petherbridge was also now studying in London, and I introduced him to my near neighbours the Abramovitzes. Deanna was very enthusiastic about Guy, partly I suspect because of his house in Greece, and they had a tryst in my studio while I was out at the cinema. Gerald was rightly enraged and Deanna, née Schwartz in South Africa, eloped as it were with Guy, living in a flat in Bayswater.

In my studio in Thurloe Square

I have talked very little about money. My father gave me enough to live on, but I was certainly not earning my own living. The paintings I sold did not contribute much to my expenses, but I had a fairly frugal life, and spent most of my time painting. It was now the 'Swinging Sixties' and my friends Geneviève and Tony Morgan were now in London working at the Indica Gallery in Masons' Yard, St. James's. The gallery was run by John Dunbar who was married to the very beautiful Marianne Faithfull who often popped into the gallery, as well as Mick Jagger, and Yoko Ono who wanted me to become part of a musical group of Cornelius Cardew. I exhibited some photographs at the gallery: collages photographed, then superimposed with other object-collages, and photographed again. John Dunbar came to my studio for a half-hour television documentary on 'Swinging London'. There was also the dress designer Jean Muir and other artists of the sixties. Even the scholarly Joseph Rykwert designed a nightclub, 'Whips' which featured fur walls and a tank of piraña fish, in the west end.

My friend David Block whom I had met in Florence was also now in London, teaching at a working men's school. He had a Turkish girlfriend, Sunay Palamutcuglari who was studying acting at RADA. David fell for a Chinese girl who was living in Holland at the time, and I saw a lot of Sunay, often going up to RADA in Brewer Street for lunch and listening to the tittle-tattle of the students. Sunay missed no opportunity to put herself forward, and was invited to dinner by Peter Hall, I think at the Dorchester, after writing to him as 'a poor little Turkish girl with her heart set on being a great actress.' In fact she won a RADA gold medal for her performance, *inter alia* in 'The House of Bernarda Alba ' of Lorca. She was a consummate liar, and on a bench in Hyde Park pretended to be Swedish to a woman stranger who was sitting there. By coincidence this woman came to my studio and Sunay's performance was revealed. Perhaps this only betokened her acting ability! She came down to Radnor, and we went to Paris together, but it was not to last, and she married a Turkish diplomat who, she told me, gave her fifty pairs of Dior shoes.

David Block had a New York friend, Mark Suckle, and togther they set up a 'Sculpture of the Month Club': an ambitious idea as it involved sending parcels to members of a sculpture every month, usually made in resin, but by interesting artists. I remember receiving these at Radnor for several months, until they fell foul of the UK customs, and we were asked to pay duty on the items.

When eventually this project came to an end, they published a series of facsimiles of books

David Block, Sunay, myself

on the subject of drugs, seminal works. We had a meeting in a club in the King's Road with a noted toxicologist, to ask his opinion. He said a large proportion of the books should be on alcohol, which was not David and Mark's idea for the series. I translated an Italian book on the production of cannabis, but did not participate further in the scheme.

Carole McCullough whom I had met in Florence was now also in London, working for a short film service in Soho, and living in a bed-sitter in Kensington. She was playing the 'cello, and at Deanna Petherbridge's flat round the corner from me, we played early music: myself on recorder, Deanna on her harpsichord, and Carole on the 'cello. This was fun, and we played once a week.

I also had a small harpsichord, or perhaps properly a spinet, by Dolmetsch, and I practised on this in my studio. However the jacks were wooden and swelled in the heating by radiator, whereas Deanna's were metal, and did not have that problem.

Most mornings I would have breakfast at a café, Dino's near South Kensington station, and I would often see an old school friend, David Methuen-Campbell who was also a painter, and lived at Redcliffe Gardens. There were now a lot of espresso bars in London, pioneered by Joseph's friend Enzo Apicella. I often saw Joseph for lunch at 'The Barile' in Harrington Road, as he was now librarian at the Royal College of Art nearby. The job was later taken by Hans Brill, Agatha Sadler's brother.

Another dear friend of that period was Dora Basilio, a Brazilian printmaker who was studying at the Slade, and had a basement flat in Eaton Terrace. She was an etcher, and entertained young artists and had good connections with galleries in Rio and San Paolo.

I had, and have, more women friends than men: I have never enjoyed the English pub life, perhaps following my father in that respect. From my school days I detested football which often seemed to be the main subject of pub conversation. I often ate at the Daquise, a Polish restaurant near Thurloe Square. It was staffed by often distinguished Polish emigrés, and one day Francis Bacon was sitting at a table and talking an American couple who asked him if he ever did sculpture. He began drawing on his napkin but of course he did not leave it behind and I only had a glimpse of what I do not think he ever made.

I would go down to Radnor every weekend, and keep an eyes on the garden and plant new seeds, and of course

Myself and Carole at the piano

Kitty, who was soon to be run over in the narrow road leading to the house, and buried under the big Cedar tree outside my studio. I was very sad about this, for a cat, he had been a very faithful companion.

Deanna went to visit Sikinos in Greece where Guy had bought a house, and she bought another. I went two or three times to Greece, first taking a boat from Venice through the Corinth canal to Athens where I met a very charming couple, the architect Loukakou and his wife who showed me the city. On the boat was Marilyn Monroe's psychiatrist, a large woman with whom I shared a table for breakfast.

I visited Deanna and Guy twice, taking the boat from the Piraeus and landing offshore at Sikinos at two in the morning. A rowing boat came to pick up the people disembarking, and then a donkey ride up to the small village. The first time I went there was no electricity on the island, and water had to be hauled up the hillside to the house from the village pump.

Guy was looking for burial mounds: there were the usual rumours of a golden calf buried on the island. But he did find an ancient coin on the beach, I believe the only one minted for Sikinos.

In the spring of of 1968 my dear father complained of pains in his back and fatigue. Doctor Hawes came up to see him and he was diagnosed with nephritis, kidney disease. He was losing weight, and was taken taken to the Royal Surrey Hospital in Guildford. He was treated in a public ward and refused a private room. I spoke to the consultant about dialysis as my father was only given a short time to live, but he turned down the idea. My mother and I transferred him to the London Clinic where he was seen by the Queen's doctor, and by Doctor Nabarro, a kidney specialist. My friend Dora Basilio was also very helpful, asking a Brazilian specialist about the problem.

The Hallway at Radnor

We visited him every day in the clinic, a rather forbidding place: in retrospect perhaps we should have taken him to King Edward VII hospital, sister Agnes's, where he was treated in the first world war.

I took him a flower of Magnolia grandiflora from Radnor, with its wonderful scent, and a bottle of Veuve Cliquot, his favourite champagne. He asked me to help him sit up in bed; he was now very weak. We had a chat about money: Ted Dew, his lawyer, had drawn up a will. He asked me to look after Marjorie and attend myself to money matters.

He had a terrible thirst, and told us he would like water from one of those Scottish burns he remembered from his childhood. We went home for the night leaving him in the care of an agency nurse. He died the next morning, on Good Friday.

He was buried at Winkfield, the family tomb of the Hercys, and his sister and other members of the family came down from Scotland. Afterwards we went back to Radnor.

I was very sad about my father's death, as it was only recently I had got to know him well. I had great respect for him and I never sought to demand anything of him, which was perhaps a mistake as he made a number of bad business decisions. Not, I may add, that I would have been much better, but we could have discussed things more, and this would have helped my mother and me after his death. As it was he made a will drawn up by his friend Ted Dew (who had been head of the Law Society School of Law.) He left Radnor and his assets to Marjorie, and then to me under the Married Women's Property Act. There were a lot of death duties to pay, nearly fifty percent, and fortunately my father had a lot of liquid money on deposit in the bank, and thus no goods or chattels needed to be sold, and not Radnor.

Marjorie with Cross at Winkfield Church   Inscription on the tomb

8

MARGARET and MARRIAGE

In January 1968, before my father had become really ill and was taken to hospital, I met an American girl, twenty-one years old, who had been in Turkey and had met a cousin of Sunay's. Her name was Margaret Sedell and she came from Oregon.

We had an instant chemistry, and talked non-stop about our lives, art, family and every other topic. It was Margaret's first visit to Europe: she was living in San Francisco at the time, having been at Mills College there. She continued her journey on to Denmark and Finland before returning to London, but in the mean time my father had died, so she never got to know him.

Margaret stayed a while, and went back to California. I missed her badly and took a flight to see her in her surroundings. She was working in an art gallery in Fisherman's Wharf and she showed me the city: we took the boat to Sausalito where we ate English fish and chips served in a specially printed English newspaper, and we drove north to Pendleton in Oregon where Margaret's father was in charge of the local airport. Margaret's parents were very hospitable and I had the feeling I was in cowboy country with the tumbleweed rolling along the roads. We saw other beauty spots like Crater Lake, and drove back through the Sequoia or redwood forests to California, passing Portland on the way.

I was sorry to leave and return to England, but Margaret promised to come to England again, which she did the next year. I introduced her to my mother and went down to Radnor. She also met my friends Joseph Rykwert and his girlfriend Paola from Italy, and Edward Wright and his wife Kitty. We also had dinner with my schoolfriend Martin Evans, now an architect and she was rather astonished to have to play word games and charades after the meal!

Margaret aged twenty-one

With Carole McCullough's help Margaret found a job in Soho at Allan King, a documentary film maker. On Saturdays we would often meet Joseph at the Caffe Torino, and do shopping at King Bomba or one of the other Italian groceries in Soho. We also saw a lot of Guy and Deanna Petherbridge, and made a trip to Sikinos where they now had two houses. They were looking for a place to live in the country, and as the stables at Radnor were now vacant, the Berridges having left, I persuaded my mother to let them rent the flat above the horse-boxes for a small rent, in return for them doing the place up, and putting in night-storage heaters. But this was later in our relationship. Margaret's father John came to London for a brief visit, and rather than be seen to be living with me she rented a room in Ovington Gardens, off the Brompton Road.

After quite a long spell in London Margaret decided to go back to California and lived in a students' apartment near the Berkeley campus with university students. I made another trip being met at San Francisco airport after stopping off in Chicago where I went to the Art Institute and saw the Picasso sculpture at the Daley Plaza.

It was fun exploring Berkeley where the aftermath of the hippy movement was still in full swing, and I met a curator of the University Art Gallery, who suggested a show with my Roman painter friend Paolo Cotani. When I got back to London I painted about ten paintings for the show in acrylic on cotton duck, and sent them rolled up for the exhibition. I never saw the show, but sold one or two of the paintings (one is illustrated here.)

I was loath to leave Margaret, and proposed that we should get married when she came back to London. She agreed, and I left in happy anticipation. However she was in trouble with the British immigration when she returned: her visa had run out, and they asked her a lot of questions about her reasons for coming to London. I had to speak to them to assure them that we were engaged to be married.

Marjorie my mother was not very happy

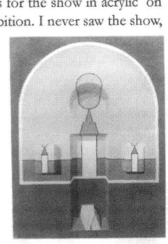

Blue sky and constructions 1970

to see her son married, the case of 'You are gaining a daughter, not losing a son!' did not occur to her. This was partly my fault as I had never really resisted her possessiveness, and of course having lost my father so recently made matters worse.

However Marjorie showed much courage in coping with her new life as a widow. In her late sixties she learnt to drive (as I had done myself a year or two earlier) and by buying a car with automatic gears she passed her driving test, and even joined a women drivers club in a nearby country house on the road to Ewhurst. She was not however a very reliable driver, and luckily she only used the car for short hops down to village. One day I was at Radnor when she walked in the front door obviously in an exhausted state, and asked for a drink. Her car had turned over in the narrow road outside our house and somehow she had managed to extricate herself none the worse for wear.

Marjorie had a great friend, April Darling, a writer, who lived with her husband a Belgian Baron near Grasse in Provence. The couple ran a nursery garden, and there was a self-contained studio on the estate which Marjorie was free to use. She often went there in the winter and painted. She had taken up painting seriously and was doing very impressionistic flower and landscape paintings, with very tentative and subtle brush-strokes. Like her father she admired Bonnard a lot, and had met his niece in Le Cannet. She also liked the work of the Ferrarese painter de Pisis who painted in somewhat the same manner.

Margaret and I made some trips to Florence and Paris, staying with

Party at Alan Shepp's studio: from left: Laurie, Alan, Carole, Deanna, Gerald, Libby, and Donna

Don and Caroline Sutphin in Florence and Geneviève Morgan in Paris who had now separated from her husband Tony, and had a pied-à-terre in the rue des Blancs Manteaux.

We visited Paolo Cotani in Rome, and were taken around the Tuscan countryside by a German amateur estate agent who showed us remote villas in 'Chiantiland' ready to be done up and fairly cheap at the time. But though we wanted to find a Mediterranean bolt-hole Margaret loved the sea and swimming, and places near the sea were already expensive. I regretted the marvellous house on Cap Ferrat that my father decided not to buy a few years before.

I was now painting larger geometrical paintings on hardboard, and also doing some cut-out sculptures of the same sort. Erika Brausen came to see this new work, but was certainly not enthusiastic. She admired much more my earlier 'surrealist' work. I also bought a 16mm Bolex cine camera and made a short animated film of the same sort of geometrical objects that I used in my paintings. This was a stop-motion film which I tried to get the Arts Council interested in, or at least to make me a small grant. Clive Tickner, a friend of Laurie Preece, helped me at least show them the film.

At Radnor Margaret and I slept in my old bedroom in the newer part of the house and my grandmother and great-aunt Jessie came to stay. Jessie became very agitated that we were sharing a room and were not yet married. She must have been about 96 years old, my grandmother a year younger. These two old girls teased each other. Once a red robin flew into my grandmother's room. Jessie was very superstitious, and said 'Oh Sarah, that's bad luck, you won't be with us much longer!' On another occasion Margaret and I drove them down to Horsham to do some shopping. We left them both in the car

Margaret and myself in a field at Radnor

with strict instructions to stay until we came back. However only my grandmother was still sitting there when we got back. "Where's Jessie?" we asked. "Oh, she went to look at the shops."

We hunted around the centre of Horsham and even went to the police, but no Jessie. Finally we made our way back the ten miles or so to Radnor, very worried as we could not imagine how Jessie would get home, or that she even knew the address. As it was she was there to welcome us at the door. It turned out that she had bought a bottle of sherry, and not wanting to admit to this misdemeanour had managed to get a taxi and find our house.

Jessie did not stay long at Radnor, and went back to her house in Plymouth, but then had to be taken into care, and died not long afterwards.

Our wedding took place on 11th.April 1970. We decided on a white wedding at the little church at Ewhurst, near Radnor. We had an earnest talk with the vicar, and posted the banns. We invited family from Scotland, and Margaret's parents, Lola and John, from Oregon. Joseph Rykwert was to be my best man, and Lynne Margaret's maid of honour. Marjorie agreed to a reception at Radnor, and a caterer arranged small tables in the 'red room', the old billiard room in the new wing of the building. We also found a small group of instrumentalists to play old music during the reception, using my small Dolmetsch harpsichord and recorders. My cousins from Scotland came down, Dora Basilio, the Perlichs, friends from Cleveland Ohio, Tony Morgan, Lo Chin Fen the jeweller from the studio below mine in Thurloe Square, Carole and Peter Smith, Rose and Lloyd, and Deanna and Guy Petherbridge.

Everyone assembled at the church in Ewhurst, Margaret and her

Wedding: from left: Marjorie, John Sedell, Lola Sedell, Myself, Margaret, Lynne, Joseph

parents had rented a car to arrive at the church from their hotel at the right time, however I had seen everyone off from Radnor and was left without transport! I finally managed to telephone the church, but Guy and Deanna had noticed that I was not at my place in the church and rushed to pick me up in their deux chevaux.

The service went well. Margaret wore a hooded gown designed by a friend of hers in San Francisco in cream silk, and made by a tailor in Horsham. There was the usual organ introit of Mendelssohn, but the bell-ringers were off duty that Saturday as it was cup-final day!

After dinner and a toast by a Scottish cousin in a kilt we went to the dining-room which had been cleared for dancing. My grandmother put in a brief appearance. Joseph came with his Italian girlfriend Paola and her little girl. We drove up to London and spent the first night of our honeymoon at the Ritz in a glamorous bedroom.

We had decided to go to Morocco for our honeymoon, via Gibraltar. We saw around the Rock and rented a car which they allowed us to take over on the ferry. It was cheaper than renting a car in Morocco.

We spent our first nights in Tangier, in a hotel where Francis Bacon always stayed, we were told. We went to a famous French café, and whom did I see at a table but Jim Wiley, the manager of Port Meirion Hotel when we lived there. I had heard that there was quite a colony of homosexuals, and my art master from Eton, Wilfred Blunt, had adventures there, also Rex Nan Kivell from the Redfern Gallery had retired there.

We had our windscreen wipers stolen in Tangier, having left the car in the road outside the hotel, and decided to be more careful in future. Not that it was raining!. We drove on to Fez, Marakech, and the foothills of the Atlas mountains. We went as far as Telouet, with its magnificent palace, Margaret driving superbly on the difficult winding mountain roads. Back in Marakech we drove into the country to a camel market and took a lot of photographs.

Our next stop was Rabat where we visited the gardens at Bouknadel laid out by a Frenchman, M François. This was a fascinating place, which

cutting the cake

comprised areas representing different areas of the world: Australia, Japan, tropical zones with lakes and bridges. François was born in Paris and told me that he was inspired by a single chestnut tree growing in the centre of a square where he lived as a child. He also had a small menagerie, but said that getting funds from the government was difficult, but I believe that now, perhaps after his death, they have taken an interest.

We went through Casablanca and back to Tangier, but poor Margaret had a raging toothache: eventually we found a dentist in Gibraltar who gave her treatment.

After our marriage we lived partly at the studio in Thurloe Square and partly at Radnor, where we ambitiously converted what had been the servants' quarters into a flat for ourselves. Needless to say Marjorie was not greatly pleased by this idea, and we had a struggle for her to let us take my piano upstairs to the new flat. We opened several small rooms into a big living-room with a fireplace and chimney in the centre. We did a lot of the work ourselves and made a kitchen where we entertained Deanna and Guy quite often, or we would go over to them for dinner.

In London we saw quite a few of Margaret's friends from the States, Richard Flagg and Connie Jump who was a Quaker and was put up at Friends' House. We also spent a Christmas with Margaret's family in Portland, also driving down to Fresno and Sacramento seeing other relations.

We also did a family tour in Scotland, staying with my uncle Doctor Dave Clark in Arbroath who was looked after by a sister and niece. He reminisced about my father, and gave me some family letters. His two sons, Cameron and Ewan were in America, one a doctor and the other a banker.

We went on to see my aunt Margaret in  h and my cousin Agnes and her husband Alastair Moncrieff at Perth. Alastair taught music at Dundee, and had a splendid Steinway piano on which he gave us a little recital of French music which he adored. He took us to the Conservative club which had an amazing assortment of whiskies.

We then went on to Glasgow and managed to go to the opera, and so back down through England.

At the studio I had a call from Annalita Marsigli. A year or two before I had taken a trip with Deanna and Gerald her husband to Ascoli Piceno in the Marche, stopping in

Studio building, 5 Thurloe Square

Bologna and visiting the Marsigli's palazzo in Via d'Azeglio where I knew Annalita's sister Isabella was living. We looked at the board with the doorbells in the courtyard, and rang. Cesena, the Marsigli's cook for whom I would go on errands when staying in Bologna, came to the door.

"Oh Signor David," she said. "You don't know what has happened!"

"No," I said. " Is the Marchese not at home?"

"There has been a terrible accident: he is dead. The Marchesa shot him!"

The story came out that Giovanni and Marlyse had had a quarrel in Milan at Isabella's flat there, and Marlyse had pulled a pistol from her handbag and shot her husband, who died in hospital a fortnight later.

When I got back to London I bought the *Corriere della Sera* every day to read about Marlys's trial in Milan. Annalita called me at the studio, very unhappy at her father's death. Marlys was condemned to prison, and then to criminal asylum which she later wrote a book about: 'La Marchesa e i demoni', her diary. She later escaped back to America and her social life as before. I heard more of the story the next time I saw Annalita in New York and Paris.

I was still painting large geometrical paintings, but had not shown them yet. Somehow I met an old school friend, Graham Hughes who was now on the board of the Goldsmiths Company, and also running the Design Centre in Neal Street. He proposed a show of my work at their gallery, but together with an American glass designer. This was a mistake: the paintings looked like a backdrop for the glassware, and I was unhappy about the result.

The next important event in our lives was a visit to Gozo, Malta.

Dave Clark, Margaret, Myself

Lo Chin Fen, the jewellery designer who had the studio under mine on the ground floor in Thurloe Square, had a friend, George Weight, who had a house in Gozo. He suggested that we rent it at Easter, telling us how beautiful the island was. We went, and were very impressed with the island, and especially the swimming which attracted Margaret greatly.

We met an amateur estate agent, Joe Said, who had already sold properties to English expatriates, and he showed us ten or so farm houses around the island.These farmhouses, often dating from the eighteenth century or before, were often reduced to complete ruin as

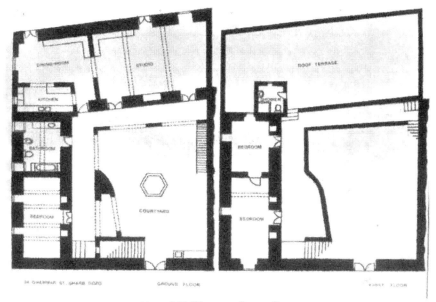

plan of 34 Ghammar Street, Gozo

younger members of farming families moved to newly-built houses in the villages.

Joe assured us that in a couple of months the houses would be done up, with modern bathrooms and kitchens, at a very reasonable price. One of the houses he showed us especially appealed: as often, it was a ruin, the animals living on the ground floor and the family above. It was in a village in the north-western part of the island, not far from a basilica named Ta Pinu, a great shrine in the island, built in romanesque style.

The house had several advantages, although there was not much of it remaining. It had a big field behind, ready to be made into a sub-tropical garden, and it was very quiet being at the end of the village of Ghammar, along a lane with a small chapel named for Saint Publius, and four or five other houses.

Next door lived an old lady, Giuseppina, who sat in the lane with her neighbour, Maria, making lace. Her brother, Luigi, had lately arrived from Detroit after working for fifty years in the automobile industry. He had not told her he was coming and to her amazement just turned up on her doorstep.

Anyway, we both loved the house and its possibilities, and although costing £4000 which was not extremely cheap at the time, with Margaret's encouragements I decided to buy it with £4000 of cash my father had left me. Of course the two months to renovate the house dragged on, as we decided to add a big living-room studio enclosing a courtyard of a good size.

The next time we came out to Gozo the work had begun on the building. An English architect friend helped, but it was largely left to the builders who had their own traditions of working with the standard blocks of stone from the quarries. We had one room to live in and a shower, and went to have breakfast every morning at the Duke of Edinburgh hotel in Victoria, the capital of Gozo, as the work started at 7 am.

We had plans for the field at the back, at present growing clover which was used to feed the cows. I planned a sort of circular pergola with eight columns supporting wooden beams. The idea being to cover the area with climbers to make shade in the summer. Our other objective was to grow subtropical plants that would be impossible at Radnor. First a windbreak was needed as the north-west wind was very strong. I planted acacias along the dividing wall of the next property, and waited for them to grow.. Also at that time relations with Colonel Gaddafi of Libya were very strong, and he presented Malta with a number of Aleppo pines which were sold for a small sum. I bought fifteen to provide shade in the garden at the back.

The summer of the next year we drove down to Malta in a Triumph Herald estate car which we had bought in England, loaded with tiles for a fountain, plants, books, canvasses. We were to take the Tyrrenia line ship from Reggio Calabria, but when we arrived there we found it was laid up for repairs, and the only alternative was to drive on to Sicily and Catania where another boat for Malta was due in two days.

We spent one night in Reggio, and then another night at a hotel in Catania. It was August and so hot we slept with our heads in the corridor of the hotel: there was not even a fan!

Building the studio-living room walls (note the thickness!)

Back garden, with lighthouse in the distance

We unloaded the car after finally arriving in Gozo, and watered the plants. In those days it was difficult to buy interesting ones there. I had a Plumbago of an exceptional blue which is still in evidence. With the plasterer from the village, Mike Saliba, I made a hexagonal fountain or pool with the Spanish tiles I had brought from London. It had an electricity point for the fountain, but over the years this gave up the ghost. Now it has fan-tailed goldfish.

In 1970 the currency was the English pound, which made life easy. There were many expatriates who were nicknamed the 'sixpenny settlers' as their tax regime was sixpence in the pound. They even organised the 'Pudding and Pie club' which met at a hotel in the little resort of Marsalforn for steak-and-kidney pie or pudding. We got to know most of these expatriates. There was Pat Holtom, a well known weaver, William Driscoll a painter and polymath who spoke many langueges including Arabic and its dialects, John Huxley and his wife who was a painter, other writers and artists.

Margaret's mother and father came to visit, and we drove back with them through Italy. The island was quite primitive in those days, almost a subsistence economy, but the Gozitans were always delightful people and many of the friends who visited us fell in love with the island, and even bought houses.

Marjorie now spent some weeks every winter in Jamaica where she had made friends. Especially the widow of Errol Flynn Patrice Wymore.

On one of these occasions Rose, the housekeeper at Radnor, telephoned me in tears to say that thieves had broken into Radnor and stolen many valuables. I decided to take the next plane to London to see what had happened, and deal with the police and insurance. I left Margaret in Gozo, and was very shocked at the story Rose told me, how she had a part-time job two days a week elsewhere, and the thieves evidently were aware of her movements and parked a van in our field and took some quite big pieces of antique furniture as well as ornaments, for example a seventeenth-century Capodimonte tankard with a scene of the descent from the Cross.

They had also removed a safe without opening it by dragging it on a rug from the first floor: fortunately there were no valuables in it. A month or two before I had taken photographs of most of the objects which was a help for the insurance, but it was a sad event, especially for Rose who took pride in looking after the house and felt responsible.

Capodimonte tankard stolen

On the way back to Gozo on the ferry I noticed an Englishman who looked as though he was new to the islands. I was astonished the next day when our bell rang and he was at the door.

It turned out that he had a friend who owned part of a farmhouse across our little lane and he was staying there without electricity or water. He was studying sculpture at the Royal College of Art in London, and his name was Brian Catling.

Brian was shortly to be married to Sue his girlfriend, and they became great friends, often coming to Gozo and camping in the empty farmhouse across the way. We saw them in London as well a lot, often at Brian's adoptive parents' house in Camberwell. In Gozo we would go for the day to the big sandy beach of Ramla, or play consequences about the local British inhabitants. Brian made two sculptures for me, one was on the roof terrace, but later had to be moved to the garden when I built another bedroom and studio upstairs. Brian's statue occasioned an extraordinary dream for me: I dreamt that a horde of mounted soldiers were coming through and looking for the True Cross, and I realised that the ten stone blocks of Brian's sculpture could form a cross. When I told him this, Brian said he had thoughts of the

Brian Catling working on sculpture

Knights Templar riding across the country, and in fact they did pass through Gozo where some were buried. Brian was astonished at my dream which corresponded with his ideas.

Brian and Sue came to Gozo quite often, staying in the farmhouse across the lane, and they came down to Radnor. We also saw a lot of Laurie and Jane Preece, and I bought two paintings of his from a show at the Redfern Gallery, portraits of the Duke and Duchess of Montefeltro, painted in grisaille as though formed from spiral binding.

Brian and myself in the garden, Gozo

I continued looking after the garden at Radnor, though Lloyd did the heavy work, mowing and digging. Our neighbour Kenneth Lee died, and a businessman, Joe Hyman, also a cotton magnate, bought the house, Lukyns, and cut down a lot of trees bounding our property to Marjorie's annoyance.

Our new living room at Radnor

One winter when Marjorie was in Jamaica a room became vacant at an old people's home, which she had approved of for my grandmother. It was a country house not far away, with a lake and swans, and comfortable rooms. We managed to take my grandmother there as it was an opportunity not to be lost, and she seemed to be very happy there, but when my mother returned she more or less accused us of kidnapping her, and she was brought back to Radnor. She died a year or so later, and was buried in Devon alongside my grandfather.

As Guy and Deanna Petherbridge were living in the flat above the stables we saw them practically every day. Deanna had a small harpsichord and played a lot of Bach, and did intricate drawings in ink of constructions in perspective which, however, was a subject she had not really studied.

We had amusing times with them, but one day they gave a party at which a young Iranian academic was present. Said boasted on this occasion that 'he only slept with married women.' I should have taken note.

Driving back from Gozo one summer we picked Marjorie up in the South of France, and stayed the night with Geneviève Morgan, who had split up from Tony, and was now living near Cézanne's house at Aix en Provence, with Patrick, an astrologer. They gave lessons in astrology and cosmology for a living.

Other expatriates in Gozo who became great friends were Tony Steven, a writer who had adapted the Galsworthy 'Forsyte Saga' for television, and had escaped to Gozo for tax reasons with his large family. He was a great raconteur, and his son Nik made films and his daughter Laurence posed for my painting 'Celestial Palestra', now in a collection in Hamburg.

Then there was Robert Scott, the son of the painter William, and his wife Anna who bought a big house in the village of Sannat, and had the intention of growing avocados for the market, but sadly the island conditions were not right.

Carol and Nina Fitzgerald probably had the most sumptuous house on the island with antique furniture and paintings, and a rarity at that time, a big swimming pool. They gave elaborate dinner parties and had two academically brilliant sons, one of whom, Edward, is a highly successful liberal barrister in London.

Gozo was still quite primitive: it could take years to have a telephone for example, and to call England we would go to the Duke of Edinburgh hotel where there was a phone booth. Your conversations could easily be overheard.

Margaret's love of swimming was helped by a Polish friend, Mick Gelbhauer who taught her diving off the salt-pans in the north east part of

Three sisters: Sarah, Millie and Jessie: grandmother and great-aunts

the island. Judy and Mick lived in the little hill-top town of Zeebug, and we saw a great deal of them.

Back at Radnor, Said Arjomand, the friend of Deanna and Guy, came to visit us quite often, and obviously took a shine to Margaret. He was an attractive man with almond-shaped eyes and curly hair, and when Margaret was in hospital for a day or two in London he brought her a lot of books of poetry. One thing led to another, and now Margaret was seeing a lot of Said, which had the result that she felt she had to decide between the two of us. She went to visit his family in Iran, and his brother in Paris.

David Russell: Italian Cinema, oil on canvas

Finally she decided in 1974 to ask for a divorce, and I went to the Queens' Bench division in the Strand with Brian Catling. My solicitor's clerk was in the row in front of me, and turned around and said "You're not going to ask for a reconciliation, are you?" I replied "Possibly!" and he said "For heaven's sake don't. You won't get your divorce if you say that!" Sure enough the judge asked that question, and I said "no your Honour, no chance of a reconciliation." The divorce was granted, and Brian took me for a drink opposite at the Wig and Pen pub, and cheered me up with a string of dirty jokes.

I was of course heartbroken at the end of our marriage. I still loved Margie, and it took me a long time to get over my sadness after she left for Chicago with overweight luggage and a tearful goodbye. She lived with Said in Chicago where he took a PHD, and she studied photography at the Art Institute. After a year or two Said sadly left her for another woman, but we kept in touch until the present day.

I have to say, however, that the tensions of living alongside my jealous mother were much to blame, and this was my fault.

Going back to Gozo was especially hard as we had made this project together, and everything in the house reminded me of her. I remember an evening at John Huxley's house when we commiserated together, as his wife had also decamped with another Gozo resident, and there was a third man also with the same history.

I threw myself into my work, and began using human figures in my paintings. I had combined geometrical elements a few years before with figures, such as in the painting 'Italian Cinema' illustrated overleaf, and at Radnor I painted 'Hommage to the King'. These two paintings opened a new era for me, and I began using models, not to paint from, but to draw and photograph.

In Gozo there was an Australian woman painter staying with a friend of hers, and she agreed to pose for dozens of photographs which I later used in my work. I began a series of paintings with three nude women in ritual scenes. I would roll these and take them to London.

David Russell: 'Hommage to the King', Oil on canvas, 127cm x 178cm

Margaret and Bacchus, Radnor

Margaret on Brighton beach

Margaret and Gunnera leaf

Myself with prickly pear, Gozo

Myself and Margaret, Gozo courtyard

House front door, Ghammar Street

Saint Publius Chapel, Ghammar Street

Maria and Giuseppina making lace in the lane

Myself as priest in Nik's film 'Fungus'

Dining room interior, Gozo

Courtyard and fountain, Gozo

9

GOZO AND RADNOR

My mother, alone at Radnor, had to decide about her future. I also had a problem: the lease on the Thurloe Square studio was coming to an end, and the landlords wanted to sell the eight studios in the building.

Marjorie asked Oliver Evans Palmer to explore the possibility of dividing the house into three or four parts, which would then be let. Of course this would pose problems of dividing the garden as well, and the project fell through: I think it would have involved too much organisation for my mother.

As for me, I could not really afford to buy the studio on a long lease, and I thought seriously about moving to France or Italy where by now I probably had more friends than in England.

In the meantime my mother had a friend with a flat in Whitelands House, a thirties apartment block in the Kings Road, near the Duke of York's barracks. She found that a small flat on the first floor was becoming available, and after having looked at other properties for sale, she took the lease of this two roomed flat.

I spent a lot of time in Gozo now, and a German painter whom I had met in London, Hans Dörflinger and his girlfriend Monika Beisner came to stay, and bought the next house to mine in the lane. And then the next house but one, another farmhouse which had been derelict a long time, and belonged to Mick and Judy Gelbhauer, was sold to David Lloyd Jones and his wife Linda. David was an architect and Linda worked at the Victoria and Albert Museum, organising their temporary exhibitions.

Although by now Malta was no longer in the Sterling Area and had her own currency, property was still cheap, and builders were becoming more accomplished at restoring the beautiful old farmhouses in the villages.

I found I worked well there with its lack of distractions, and I felt at home in the mediterranean climate.

From Malta it was easy to get to Sicily, and I took a bus tour of five days around the island. We stopped the nights in Jolly hotels, and it was a convenient way of seeing Segesta, Piazza Armerina, Selinunte, and the other temples, ending up in a Danish hotel with Danish food and magazines on the tables, and a totally Danish clientele apart from one excessively tall Englishman called Metcalfe, a relation of the famous 'Fruity'.

Another visit from Malta was to Tunisia where I had made arrangements with Brian and Sue that I would meet them at a big hotel on the coast at Sousse at a certain hour in the evening.

With my suitcases I waited and waited but they did not turn up, and I was beginning to get quite frantic. I certainly did not want to roam around Tunisia on my own. It was quite late when I decided to head back to the town centre and book in at the nearest small hotel. But to my dismay there was no room anywhere. I did not want

Myself, Sue and Brian in Kerkennah island, Tunisia

to sleep on the beach with my suitcases as pillows, so I walked out of the town centre again. I finally found a seedy place, 'Hotel Moderne' with a dirty creaking bed and the door to the lavatory permanently open I left early in the morning. I had a back-up rendez vous with Sue and Brian at the entrance to the Souk. But I found that the Souk had several entrances, but I sat at a café near what I thought was the principal one. I managed to get a Daily Telegraph to read, but was pessimistic about the possibility of meeting my friends. However, after an hour or so they found me. I was greatly relieved. They had found a hotel for the night, and were ready to explore the country.

In Tunis was had a strange experience; we sat in a small public garden eating sandwiches, but noticed people giving us dirty looks. A policeman came up to us and ordered us out of the garden: it turned out that it was only for use by women and children. We rented a small car and drove south, hoping to see the Sahara desert. We stopped in Sfax where we were accosted by a Mr. Barbara who was a Maltese who had never been to Malta. He had a room to let for the night, and he asked us to follow him some paces behind. Probably he had no right to rent the room. But it was fine, and he made a big breakfast for us the next day, proudly showing us his Maltese passport. One day he would like to go there.

We drove on south to Gabes where we had a camel ride in the oasis, and then to Tozeur, a beautiful city with its decorative brickwork. We had our first glimpse of the desert, and decided to cross the great Chott or salt lake the next day to Matmatah. To do this however we needed a guide as there was no obvious road on the Chott, and in the hotel we found Mohammed who agreed to accompany us across and then return on his own.

That evening he invited us to dinner at his house, which was taken in the courtyard in front of a televison, sitting on the ground. Girls arrived with trays of delicious food.

After crossing the Chott, the hotel at Matmatah was extraordinary, consisting of rooms carved in a sort of quarry below ground level. Very cool in the summer heat, and strange breakfasting the next day at the same table as a Swiss advertising executive.

After some adventures on the road we spent a night on the island of Kerkennah, taking the ferry from Sfax. From Tunis we took the ferry to Trapani in Sicily, and stayed with friends in Palermo. Brian was eager to vitit the catacombs. A monk who looked like Father Christmas showed us into the eerie tombs. Due to the dry air the bodies and clothes were well preserved, some sitting up and some, like the children who were wearing crowns, lying down on sort of shelves. We had not finished looking around when suddenly the lights went off and this was quite terrifying. Father Christmas called down to us that he was closing up and we managed to find our way out.

Back in London I saw alot of Laurie and Jane Preece and Brian and Sue Catling. I was doing some writing as well: a sort of holiday from painting. I wrote two novels, 'A Voice of Wax and Parchment', and 'Three May Keep a Secret', the former a search for buried paintings by Raphael, and the second a thriller set in Italy about a murderous child. Neither was published, although I had an agent who liked the books, but was unable to find a publisher. I tried my schoolfriend Adrian House who was now at Collins, but he found difficulties with one of the books. While I was still with Margaret we also saw a lot of an American couple, Alex Gross and his wife Ilene Astrahan. He was a writer, a sort of polymath and linguist whom I had met in Florence, and she was a Magic Realist painter who later turned to computer art. When in 1972 Alex was in New York he met the publisher of 'Arts Magazine' at an exhibition opening. The

Myself in Gozo

publisher happened to be looking for a new London correspondent as Patrick Heron, the painter, who had been doing the job, had quit. Alex mentioned me, and I sent a specimen article and was hired to write every month, with photographs, many of which I took myself. This was fascinating, and I found that I was more welcome in the galleries as critic than as painter.

My father's inheritance was now proving a problem. My mother was to enjoy the house for her lifetime, and then it would be passed to me, as well as the capital in shares and deposit accounts that my father left. We ended up employing three lawyers, one for my mother, one for myself, and one for the estate. My mother wanted to spend the capital that was left in trust and also sell Radnor. I could understand her wishes, but did not want to contemplate the idea of selling the house.

For probate reasons we had all the chattels in the house valued by Christies, and we jointly decided to sell some of the paintings. There was a Hoppner portrait, a Dahl, and a Gainsborough of Mrs.Elizabeth Uvedale from his Sudbury days.

Nattier: Duc d'Orleans

The Gainsborough was bought by Agnews, and the other paintings fetched reasonable prices. We decided to keep two important paintings: a Nattier portrait of the Duc d'Orleans, and a Siennese Madonna by Fungai. The sitting room did not look the same also with the absence of the stolen furniture and porcelain.

I was still keeping an eye on the garden, especially the dozen or so species of Eucalyptus which were now growing into fine trees. I was always worried about the effect of the cold on these however, but so far there were no casualties. One sad casualty however was a Cornus nuttallii, the mountain dogwood, which was a fine tree that Mr. Shrub of Hilliers had wanted to buy. Michael Haworth Booth also came to give us advice, being a great advocate of mulches for the rhododendrons and other rare shrubs. I grew several varieties of bamboo, and cut some pieces for a big curtain in Gozo which divided the living room, or studio as it was then, from the dining-room.

For my fiftieth birthday I gave a big party at Radnor, inviting Deanna and Guy of course, and an artist who I was fond of, Angela Gorgas, but who was the fiancée of Martin Amis. Laurie and Jane brought their children, Lola, Georgia

Gainsborough, Mrs. Elizabeth Uvedale

and Daniel. Unfortunately the children had chickenpox although they were not showing the spots yet, and embracing them to thank them for a birthday present I caught the illness. I was confined to the house for about a month, but it had the good effect of curing me of my habit of smoking which had become quite alarming. I no longer felt like a cigarette, and have never smoked since.

My mother was now spending a lot of time in the flat in London, as well as taking trips to stay with her friends near Grasse, or going to Jamaica. The flat, though small, had a big terrace looking onto the Kings Road, and in the summer was quite pleasant to sit outside for a drink, looking over the road to the Chelsea Kitchen, a reasonably priced restaurant where she often had a meal and chatted to people. I remember having lunch there with Marjorie and her friends the actors Esmond Knight and Nora Swinburne. Marjorie also bought clothes at Peter Jones nearby and knew the shopgirls well. She still saw a lot of Clive Lythgoe and his partner Jean François Giuliani. She made friends easily, chatting up people and getting their addresses. The adjoining flat to hers at Whitelands House belonged to Maidie Weizmann, the daughter-in-law of the Israeli president, and they became very friendly, except for the fact that Maidie would knock on my mother's door too early in the morning with a cup of tea. Maidie was a doctor, and still practised.

The time sadly came when there seemed to be no choice but to sell Radnor. The house was obviously too big for my mother, and I also felt lost there now I was alone, apart from my friends Deanna and Guy still living above the stables. Marjorie spoke to Knight Frank and Rutley about a price

Myself, cousin Neto Hunter, Margaret, and Uncle George Mochrie in Gozo

for the house which would of course include the stable block and the tied cottage adjoining it. There was the usual advertisement in Country Life magazine, but it resulted in few, if any, replies. I do not think my mother had thought of the logistics of moving from such a big house, and although she still had in mind the idea of buying another place, perhaps in France, the only possibility was to store all the furniture if the house was sold.

In the event the sale of Radnor was due to the local postman. When delivering letters to Hurtwood House, our neighbours on the hill which was now a school, he mentioned to the owner, Mr Jackson that our house was for sale. At last someone was interested, and the house was sold in 1977 for a reasonable price at the time.

Coincidentally, around the same time, my studio in London was sold to a property company. I could have bought a new lease or the freehold, but it was more than I could afford, so I had to move my paintings and small amount of furniture back down to Radnor.

All the contents of Radnor was sent to David Mann in Cranleigh, our nearest small town, which was a furniture shop and store whom we had dealt with for many years. Before doing so my mother and I had to agree on the division of possessions, and this was not easy. There were other problems: the Lloyds who lived in the tied cottage had to leave, and be compensated, Deanna and Guy also. The statue of Bacchus and other garden ornaments were sold to Crowther of Sion House. I would have liked to take the statue to Gozo, but it would have been an impossible cost.

The day of moving Brian Catling came down to comfort me, much as

The drawing room, Radnor

he had done at my divorce: this was an equally sad parting for me. I had spent years working in the garden, buying shrubs and trees which were now maturing, building up a library, and painting. For years afterwards I would dream about the house and what had happened to it, sometimes finding hidden rooms, or new exotic plants which were either flourishing or dying. I have only been back once when Laurie Preece drove me past the house. The old kitchen garden was now built over with ugly small houses, and the field we used to call 'Scotland' was no longer a field with its ferns and ponds. I could hardly bear to open my eyes, and we did not stop.

Laurie had now bought a house in North Wales, very near Maes-y-Neuath where I had lived during the war, and I managed to to give him some shrubs from Radnor, which he also planted where they lived in Wandsworth. Others I was able to take to Gozo, for example Yucca gloriosa which had in its turn come from the factory garden at Merton.

Myself, Margaret and Laurie Preece

I drove Marjorie down to the South of France to look for properties, as she was still thinking of buying a house somewhere, and we went to agents in Nice, talked to her friend the widow of Nubar Gulbenkian who lived near Grasse, but I had the impression that my mother was not really serious. We saw a beautiful town house in St Remy de Provence for example, which seemed very cheap, but she could not decide: indecisiveness was a failing she suffered from frequently!

I decided I would have to be more decisive for myself, as I now had to find somewhere at least to store my books and paintings. Of course I had the house in Gozo, but could not contemplate living there year round.

I took the train to Paris and had a look at the possibility of renting a large flat. I went to Versailles and made an appointment to see over an apartment on the Grand Avenue. I waited for the agent but she did not turn up, and I gave up the half-hearted search.

I decided to make my way to more familiar ground, viz Florence, and took the train down, and called Don and Caroline Sutphin when I got there.

Laurie as boxer

111

It appeared that Caroline had tried to call me as there was an amazing apartment in the offing. It was owned by the uncle of their own landlord, Count Recco Capponi, in Via de Bardi. They lived at no.36, and this flat was the *piano nobile* at no 28, the Palazzo Canigiani. It measured about 300 m², and looked onto the Arno at the back. There was a doctor or lawyer after it, so Caroline was keeping her fingers crossed that it was still available. I went to have a look. It was extraordinary, around a courtyard attributed to Michelozzo, and consisting of four big reception rooms, a *tinello* or kitchen-dining room, two bedrooms, one with a communicating loo, and an antiquated bathroom with tiles that must have dated from some previous century.

The rent was so small that I decided it would be even worth renting just to store my chattels. And besides I knew Florence well, and loved Italy.

Caroline made a date for lunch at 'Le Sorellé', a trattoria nearby , and when I arrived she and Don had a bottle of spumante on the table. Caroline said "You've got it!" I said "I've got what?" not thinking. She said "The apartment!" The prospective tenant had complained about the ancient tiles in the bathroom, and as Don and Caroline were already tenants of the family, they were prepared to offer the flat to me. I was overjoyed of course, and could hardly believe my luck. So began my exile!

The Courtyard attrib. Michelozzo, Palazzo Canigiani

Adolescent Games Oil on canvas 102 cm x 127 cm

Purple Smoke Oil on canvas 102 cm x 127 cm Private Collection London

Punishment of a Princess Oil on canvas 102 cm x 127 cm

The Red Box Oil on canvas 102 cm x 127 cm Private Collection France

10

BELLA ITALIA

I went back to England, and explained to my mother my intentions, also to my friends. I would have to make arrangements for removals of my furniture and paintings to Florence which would be a big undertaking, and deal with any other bureaucracy that the move entailed, and consult my lawyer, Count Piccolomini.

I left a lot of my work in store at Mann's in Cranleigh, and agreed with my mother what furniture I should take, including, for example, the piano.

I left London driving down with Laurence Steven, Nik's sister, stopping two nights on the way at Chantilly and Aosta. I was counting on my Florentine friends to help me with the logistics of the move as there would be a very big removals van which had to park on the lungarno outside the gates of the palazzo. A local firm was going to provide a small shuttle van to go from the street to the back gate of the palazzo, less than a hundred yards, but nevertheless necessary.

Two great friends of mine were Antonio Masi and Grazia Zatti, and Grazia was very efficient at organisation, also Don and Caroline Sutphin.

The day arrived of the delivery and we lined up three cars on the lungarno which would be driven off when the English removal van arrived. This manoeuvre worked well, and Grazia stood on the tailboard of the van directing operations. There was a small lift to the first floor which could be used for smaller items, but everything else including big wardrobes, tables and beds had to be carried up the two flights of stairs. The piano was something of a problem as the local removal men did not have the right equipment for moving pianos, but somehow succeeded in the end. The next day Neri and Flavia Capponi came in to have a look at my library spread out on the floor of the biggest *salone*.

I was soon inviting my friends to visit me: Geneviève and Patrick, Brian and Sue, my mother who was rather indignant that I had so many objects from Radnor, and my English solicitor Trevor Milne-Day who recommended a friend of his, Sarah MacCready who was going to be studying painting at Signora Simi's academy for some months, to rent a room in the enormous flat.

I started painting and writing, and arranging my books. With my friends we had the habit of lunching at *Le Sorelle*, so named because of the three sisters who owned the trattoria. Don Sutphin especially lunched there as his studio was nearby in an incredibly rural setting for the centre of Florence, on Via Erta Canina.

In the summer I would take the train to Rome and a flight to Malta, where I would pick my car up at a garage in Birzebugia near the sea. I invited Joseph and his new wife Anne and her daughter Marina for a month one summer. Joseph who was teaching at Essex University made a photographic record of the neolithic temples in Malta and Gozo for the university archives. There was a local architect whom Joseph said had been pestering him, and whom he did not want to meet, but he was at a formal dinner so Joseph was obliged to say hello.

In those days, before I had a swimming pool, we went nearly every day to the sea, either the sandy beach of Ramla, or one of the many small bays where the swimming was good, and still unspoilt by tourism.

Joseph and Anne Rykwert, with Marina in my courtyard

Paolo Cotani, the Roman painter came with his wife and I met them at the airport: however they were accompanied by another three people, including a Duchess, and I explained that I did not have room for so many people. Paolo said "Well, they can stay in a *pensione!*" I then had to explain that there were no *pensioni* that I knew of, as in those days there was very little hotel accommodation at all in Gozo. Luckily I was able to put them up in a house of a friend, Charles Denton, in the village.

The principal meeting place in Victoria, or Rabat, the capital of the island, was the Duke of Edinburgh hotel, which had the only public telephone for making long distance calls, but this could unfortunately be overheard by guests sitting in the lounge. One of the habitués of 'The Duke' was Tony Steven, the father of Nik the film maker whom I have mentioned before as being a writer and tax exile. We would also hang out at the Barbarella, an open-air disco, or the Sesame in Gharb where Tony would often end the evening passing out with too much whisky and having to be carried home.

In the early 1970s I painted a lot in Gozo, rolling the paintings to take back to Florence. In those days there were customs problems with works of art, but with the European Union these gradually disappeared. However I had to pay a considerable sum bringing my possessions into Malta, the only concessions being for potential residents. I later became a permanent resident of Malta, and could bring my effects in freely.

In Florence Sarah MacCready left after her term at Signora Simi's academy was over, and I found another tenant, Michèle Zamfiresco who was working at Meli the jeweller on the Ponte Vecchio. Her father was Romanian but she was born in France, and had been living in Florence with an English antique dealer, but they had separated recently. Michèle helped me a lot in the house, and stayed for more than five years, while various girlfriends of mine came and went. One of these was Anne Deneys whom I met when she was an au-pair with Anna Scott in London. She had studied at the Ecole Normale Supérieure in Antony near Paris, and applied for a scholarship at the European University at San Domenico near Florence.

An extremely bright student she was accepted by two faculties, and at first moved in with me. Her father was professor of philosophy at Nice, and her mother a concert pianist.

Monika and Pat with sheep in the lane

Michèle had a Dutch friend who worked in the fashion business, and his colleagues in Amsterdam were two sisters, the daughters of Bob Haak the director of the Historical Museum there, and a great expert on Rembrandt. I had always wanted to go back to Amsterdam, and we did a swap: the Haak family came to Florence for a month, and I stayed in their house on the Prinzengracht, which boasted a Steinway piano and an elderly cat who had to be let out on the tiles every day, and of course fed.

I invited Brian and Sue for a week to Amsterdam. The Haaks had a small motorboat tied up near the house on the canal, and Brian bravely got it going and we sped around Amsterdam narrowly missing other boats, and passing by the Rijksmuseum.

We rented a car and went to the Hague, Haarlem, Leyden,and Delft where we recognised scenes from Herzog's 'Dracula'. We also went night-clubbing, and I had the idea for, and began writing, an illustrated erotic novel.

I was very moved by Anne Frank's house, and burst into tears in the street after leaving. This has not happened to me very often, but it happened on another occasion in Amsterdam when I first saw the 'Night Watch'.

I took back two souvenirs from Amsterdam, a brass four- branched candlestick and a pottery bowl made by friends of the Haaks.

A great friend in Florence was Tony Mathews whom I had met with Robert and Anna Scott. Tony was working with Idea Books, a publishing firm, mostly of art books, in Milan, directed by Alvise Passigli who had a big house in Fiesole, near which Tony also bought a house later on.

Salone, Via de Bardi 28, Florence

My book was entitled 'Sophie's Dream Book', and had twenty full-page erotic pen and ink drawings. With Tony's help Idea Books agreed to distribute it, although it was published under the name of Mountjoy Editions, Florence. Setting up the text was quite complicated as the compositors did not know English, and there were about thirty mistakes per page from the typescript manuscript. However there was also an Italian edition, translated by Maria Grazia Zatti, and this was easier for them. The text was printed in Florence, but the binding was done in Bologna, in red cloth with endpapers

Before distribution the police turned up at the printers to approve the publication, and went away with signed copies.

The edition was 300 copies, all signed by the author, and now, if they can be found in a bookshop, are quite expensive. Signora Bellini in Milano stocked the book in her erotic bookshop, and I went to New York for a show of the illustrations at the Erotics Gallery, run by Edie Solow. She became a good friend and put me up in New York. I had, however, a contretemps with the US customs as the books had been labelled as educational by Idea Books, and a customs officer had a look, and banned them pending inspection by the authorities.

All was well after a phone call to the censorship authority who explained that if the books had been works of art, containing hand-printed illustrations for example, there would have been no problem. The book would be released but too late for the opening of my exhibition unfortunately.

I saw a number of friends in New York, including David Block who had married with two children, and was living in Connecticut and dealing in antiquarian books. His wife was Chinese and at the beginning of their marriage there was some friction between David's orthodox Jewish family and Shiumin's aristocratic Chinese family. But all seemed resolved with the birth of their first child.

David and Shiumin Block with Anya and Ezra

I also saw Bruce Winston and Annalita who had written a play performed off-Broadway. She had a big duplex apartment on Riverside Drive, and I met her niece, her sister Isabella's daughter. She had divorced her doctor husband, and was about to marry a rich English writer and Japan guru, Ivan Morris. He fell ill two weeks before the marriage in Bologna, and Annalita inherited a beautiful small château near Paris where she lived for a while, and where I visited her on a trip to Paris, staying at a small flat she had near the Parc Montsouris.

I had quite a social life in Florence. My old friend Baronessa Scaglione invited me to her soirées and dinner parties where I met many of the old Florentine families: the Antinoris, the Ginoris, the Rucellais and Ricasolis. At one dinner party we were seated at little round tables with exquisite lace tablecloths, and I was with Contessa Ricasoli and two or three others, and it was time for the coffee. Livia's butler served the coffee in little decorated cups, but I did not realise they were papier maché and the coffee spilled all over the table. Livia Scaglione was also a friend of another Englishman, Julian Grenfell, who was an old Etonian and I went to his wedding reception after his marriage at Poggio Imperiale.

I also saw a lot of John Phillips who had become very friendly with Marjorie, and saw her in Los Angeles, after she had stayed with Clive Lythgoe and Jean-François Giuliani in New York. He also came to Gozo while she was there.

'Sophie's Dream Book' although in a limited edition of 300 copies, was a success as far as it went. Playboy TV did a spot with me, inviting a dozen people for drinks at my flat. Richard Fremantle, an art historian who lived at the top of a tower on the other side of the river, was there, and oif course Michèle and other friends. I contacted Karl Ludwig Leonhardt from Hamburg who was interested in doing a German version of the book, but this came to nothing. However I made an important contact in London, Jamie Maclean, an old Etonian who had had a gallery of erotic art in Mayfair, and was now in the publishing business with his partner Tim Hobart.

Back in Florence Anna Scotti gave me an introduction to Camillo d'Afflitto who had opened a gallery in Via degli Albizzi called Vività. At the time he was having a show of art deco furniture, but he was interested in my work and introduced me to a friend, Piero Lorenzoni who had a large collection of erotica, books and photographs. Piero was from Trieste and taught history of art at the Accademia delle Belle Arti in Florence. He in turn introduced me to a journalist, Ilaria Galli who turned up at Via de Bardi to interview me, and became one of my greatest friends to this day.

Ilaria Galli

A year or two later I painted four portraits of her, in the four seasons, painting 'Summer' when she was visiting me in Gozo, and 'Winter' in Florence, wearing an astrakhan coat.

Ilaria was a great bibliophile and introduced me to some of the antiquarian dealers in Florence who stocked my book. The Biblioteca Nazionale which had its seat in Florence also bought a copy of 'Sophie.'

Camillo d'Afflitto invited me to contribute to a big erotic exhibition at his gallery: 'Eros e la Gioia di Vivere.' The gallery comprised a number of large spaces and I showed several large paintings which I worked on in Florence and Gozo (see plates V and VI.) There were photographs, sculpture, and a passageway with a grating in the floor with a wind machine below which blew up women's skirts as they walked over it, like the Marilyn Monroe film 'The Seven Year Itch.'

The show received a lot of notice in the press, and in fact was one of the first big erotic exhibitions in Europe. The next big exhibition was 'Erotica 92' organised by Clive Griffiths in Bologna, but more of that later.

Mentioning Bologna I forgot to mention a trip in the early sixties to visit the painter Giorgio Morandi. A friend living in Florence, Lys McClaughton, had an invitation from the great painter. She had written to him and was surprised to receive a reply. Lys asked me to come along as she spoke very little Italian. We took a bus to Via Fondazza 36 and a young maid opened the door on the first floor. We met Morandi's white-haired sister and Morandi came in. He offered us American cigarettes, his favourites he said. He smoked a great deal. He was not what I expected: from his work I expected someone retiring and shy, but he was full of energy and talked a lot about Bologna and mutual friends like Salvatore Fiume.

David Russell: Portrait of Anne Deneys

He showed us what he was working on, and it turned out that Lys had a commission from a gallery to buy a painting for a New York gallery. I was rather annoyed about this as it was such an honour to talk to the great man without a commercial undercurrent. In the event she bought two drawings: Morandi said all his paintings were committed to the Galleria del Milione and he had only drawings to sell, and would I also like to buy one for about £30 at the time. I had no money on me and because I had not come for that reason I declined, and have regretted it ever since! Returning to Florence I wrote a full account of my visit, so far unpublished, but too long to quote here.

A friend I had met in Gozo with his very young girlfriend was Ivan Alechine, the son of Pierre Alechinsky the painter. Alexandra, his girlfriend, introduced two young girls who were coming to study at the Belle Arti, and I said I would put them up, at least until they were settled. One was French and the other from the Ivory Coast and they slept in my studio for a while. Then a model Kathleen Michael came to stay after I had made a lot of drawings of her. She was from San Francisco and later came to Gozo with a French painter who called herself Galatée de Brunswick. These two stayed quite a while when Michèle was still renting a room. I made a Christmas card of them posing like two children in front of a copy of a Canova statue which I brought from England.

Kathleen and Galatée Christmas card

Since childhood when I made Christmas cards every year for my parents, I continued the practice and a number of friends have collected them from year to year. Later on in Florence I made etchings with the help of the printer Vittoria Pozzi.

Another Florentine activity was singing madrigals. Susan Arcamone, an American who worked at I Tatti, the Berenson villa at Settignano, and Candace Adelson an art historian specialising in tapestry, were instrumental in setting up the group which originally met at Susan's flat, but later moved to my salone which afforded a piano and more space. We were usually six or eight singers, sometimes more or less and we sang madrigals from different periods and countries, on occasion interpreting scores that had not had an airing for several centuries. We sang madrigals from France, Germany, Italy and England: Arcadelt, Marenzio, Gibbons, de Lassus and the more difficult Gesualdo and Monteverdi. The presence of singers varied from week to week and was somewhat lacking in Italians who were not used to amateur singing of this kind. We usually had something to eat after an hour or two singing, and this became something of a social occasion.

Later on the Anglican bishop of Florence joined us, and I turned around any overly erotic paintings although he had been a priest in Soho so was not probably schockable. In the last year or so I was in Florence we sang at the bishopric in Via dei Serragli. We gave several recitals, especially at I Tatti. I enjoyed this musical exercise enormously, and miss it now. I am just left with a big box of xeroxed parts. Here in France there does not seem to be an easy way of joining a madrigal group, although I am sure they exist.

I saw a great deal of Antonio Masi and his partner Grazia Zatti. They lived nearby and kindly invited me often for dinner. Grazia and I would go shopping at the supermarket Esselunga once a week. However later on Antonio and Grazia separated, and she rented John Phillips's old apartment in Palazzo Giucciardini when John moved first to the south of France, and then to Vevey in Switzerland.

In the early days of living in Florence I had a lot of visitors from England, France, Gozo and other places. In Gozo I had met Ann Monsarrat the wife of the novelist Nicholas Monsarrat. Nicholas died and Ann began to lead a more social life. Later in the nineteen eighties she came to Florence, and with other friends we took the train, in our carnival costumes, to Venice, but more of that later. In 1980 Michèle and I organised a big carnival party in the flat. The theme was Venice and we arranged a stall with Venetian lanterns for a roast suckling pig, in the form of a gondola, not full size but quite big, a tableau of Titian's 'Sacred and Profane Love' with Susan Arcamone and Candace Adelson as the protagonists, a Venetian friend reading from Goldoni in dialect, and of course Venetian food. And there was Kathleen doing exotic, if not exactly Venetian, belly-dancing.

The idea originally was eighteenth century Venice, but this turned out to be quite difficult to adhere to, so there were gondoliers, Venetian blinds, the Venice rugby team (this friend was adept at ousting gatecrashers at the door,) Marco Polo (Marina Orloff Davidoff), one or two *bauta* masked figures, a prisoner (Don Sutphin) from the *Piombi* jail, and the inevitable Casanovas.

I suppose there were a hundred or so guests at the party which went on until the small hours and was a success. At one point Harold Acton turned up, but not in costume, and said how much he liked to see young people enjoying themselves. A boyfriend of his had been invited. Below myself with my dottoressa, Laura Lanza, the daughter of the director of the Florence Natural History Museum.

We were so pleased with the result of this party that Michèle and I decided to do another the next year with the theme of Science Fiction. This was even more elaborate with a local band whom Michèle had heard practising in a basement in Via de Bardi and who agreed to come along in return for dinner. We tried to find spooky science fiction music, like the Doctor Who theme. The band later became very famous in Italy as Litfiba.

This time there were several hundred guests and two architects were shaking their heads as the centuries old beams of the salone floor seemed to be bouncing . We had to restrict the numbers dancing at one time.

Another idea we had in the end

Laura Lanza and myself, carnival party

fell through. The idea was to auction a young girl who would then proceed with her new owner to the planet Eros, which was a small closed room, with a closed circuit television that could be seen by guests outside. A young French girl volunteered for this rôle, but backed out at the last minute.

Otherwise we made 'space food', for example blue pasta which the Italians were very reluctant to try, and there were many ingenious costumes, for example a black hole, and a toxic cloud, the latter worn by Tony Mathews and which caught fire, luckily to be put out in time by Mercury (Susan Arcamone.)

Invitation to Fantascienza party, February 1981

We hired a 16mm projector to show a rather poor nineteen seventies sci-fi film, and my costume was a two-headed monster (one head above the other) and a detachable penis which everyone wanted to pull off.

Myself as sci-fi monster

Guests came to the party from the US, England, France, Malta, but the problem was that it was difficult to identify individuals under their costumes, and there were one or two thefts in spite of having tried to put valuables away. We decided that this would be the last big carnival party at Via de Bardi, and in future years I went to Venice with a new (hired) costume.

Amazingly no one in the building complained of the noise, although upstairs lived the distinguished art historian John Pope-Hennessy. The walls of the building were however very thick but the collapse of the floor could have been a

122

disaster. Fortunately the old timbers and tiles stood their ground. Some enthusiasts started a body painting session, and quite a few romances started that evening by all accounts.

I made regular trips to London to see my mother, and one Christmas took a package tour with Ilaria staying at a hotel near South Kensington. This was amusing as we took a bus from Dover with a complement of Italians hoping to do a lot of shopping, however the tour guide on the bus patiently explained that in London the shops, cinemas and theatres were all closed over Christmas. There was the sad spectacle of enthusiastic Florentines milling around with nowhere to go. With Marjorie we went to Kew Gardens and Fortnum and Mason's, and the theatre.

Ilaria also came to Gozo where her big hats and high heels created a sensation in the village. Although almost everyone in Malta spoke Italian

Sir Harold Acton and Charles Pillans

it was not often they saw anyone like Ilaria in Gozo. Perhaps a figure from a Fellini film was the nearest equivalent. We had lunch with Joe Demajo, a wealthy businessman whose wife Teresita was from Padua. They of course spoke Italian, and got on well. Ilaria rented a typewriter and a young German child, a neighbour, would sit spellbound watching Ilaria at work.

Ilaria and Marjorie in Marjorie's London flat

Susan Loewenherz was an American sculptress now living in Florence with her son Franz. She was working on erotic pieces in Carrara, where she later went to live and marry Paolo Grassi, a marble mason from the town. Piero Lorenzoni had the idea of a big show of erotic art at the Forte Belvedere in Florence, and invited us to contribute, as well as one or two other artists including Silvio Santini, another sculptor friend of Susan.

One of the paintings I exhibited was the 'Ecstasy of Saint Theresa'. Ilaria had posed as a model for this painting, with Susan's son Franz as the Angel. It was obviously influenced by Bernini's sculpture, with some erotic elements. Silvio's sculpture was brilliant: a marble bed with a counterpane leaving a gap beneath where you could put your hand to feel an erect marble organ ready to enter a marble woman's body. These were realistically carved, but could not be seen, only felt.

Myself working on Saint Theresa

Other paintings I exhibited in this show had already been seen in 'Eros, Gioia da vivere.' 'Tentazioni' caused some stir in Florence and attracted a big public.

Not all my friends approved my interest in erotic subjects, but the title of a short critique of my work by Brian Catling in later years gives the idea of what I was trying to do: 'The Geometry of Desire.'

Ritual, Egyptian art, and above all the art of Ancient Greece attracted me. I also was interested in neo-classicism, David for example, and Ingres, and around this time I met a friend of Michèle's, Vittoria Pozzi, who was working as a lithographic printer, but then opened her own premises in the centre of Florence to print etchings and engravings. She reprinted some of the plates I had etched in England, but I did many more in her studio, in small editions. One of these was 'Noctes Luxuriae' a set of six folio scenes with stories attached, and another was 'Ganesh and the Egyptian Princesses', much later. I enjoyed working in the studio, meeting other artists, for example Silvio Loffredo and Luca Alinari. In the early nineties Laurie Preece came down and Vittoria printed an edition of his aquatints 'Illuminations.'

My next big project, again with the help of Anthony Mathews, was a pop-up book. I am not sure where I got the idea for this, but an erotic pop-up book seemed a natural, and I started learning paper engineering, self-taught by taking apart various children's pop-ups.

The subject of the book was the carnival in Venice, and featured Arlecchino and Columbina, a Venetian Marchese, gondoliers, an erotic scene in Piazza San Marco. The most complex of the seven scenes was a gondola emerging from under a bridge, the gondolier standing up to be embraced by a nude girl straddling the prow.

The book took a great deal of work, approximating all the moving parts until everything worked by pulling tabs, or opening and closing the book. Anthony took the maquette to Signora Bellini in Milan who had a contact with World Books in America. At the time the leading manufacturer of pop-up books was in Columbia, but they employed young girls who objected to the erotic material. The World Books representative took the maquette to Taiwan, and other countries, but it seemed impossible to find a source that would produce the book at a reasonable price.

In the end I showed the book to Jamie Maclean and Tim Hobart in London who had already given me a small show of my paintings at their premises in Drayton Gardens, off the Fulham Road. Jamie was very enthusiastic, and after much deliberation agreed to publish a limited edition of three hundred copies, providing it would be possible to deal with the logistics of manufacture and binding.

The first thing to do was to prepare sheets of the different parts of each page so that dies could be made to cut out the sections.

I found a firm at Caravaggio, near Bergamo, who specialised in making dies: essentially blades curved to the outlines of the drawings, and set into sheets of plywood. These would then be used in a special machine to cut the various pieces that made up the pages. This latter stage would be done in London.

So I took the sheets to Caravaggio, and the dies were made and shipped to London. But the black-and-white sheets would have to be printed by lithography, and then hand-coloured. Laurie Preece helped me find a printer who taught at the Brighton art college, and he printed the sheets on the necessary stiff card, and a firm was found to cut out the parts ready to be coloured and glued.

'The Secret Carnival,' my pop-up book

But who was to do the hand colouring? Jamie managed to find

three girls, art students, who were prepared to come to his house and colour the printed sheets by hand. The whole was supervised by John Reyntiens, the son of the famous stained glass artist. I made a short video to show him how the gluing could be done in half-an-hour.

I found a reasonably priced binder in Florence who bound the majority of the books in a green cloth, and a few in red which were to be a sort of de luxe version which would be sold with an original drawing of mine relating to the Venetian Carnival. The book was now entitled 'The Secret Carnival,' and Jamie Maclean collaborated on the small amount of text in the book. Jamie gave a party for the launching of the book, and quite a number were sold. Many years later, in Christie's Paris sale of Gérard Nordmann's collection of erotic books, the de luxe edition sold for more than 1000 euros.

Myself and Ann Monsarrat in Venice

In 1986 I went to the revived carnival in Venice with Ann Monsarrat. We were joined by Hans Dörflinger and Monika Beisner coming from Constanz in local bird costumes. . We travelled by train from Florence in costume: in the carriage were other revellers in costume including a bumble bee. For several days we paraded around Venice, Ann acting as my page and clearing the way for our progress. We even went to museums and restaurants in costume, and one of the highlights of the visit was 'Il Serraglio' of Mozart at the Fenice. The orchestra were also in costume, and there were a number of French visitors in Napoleonic outfits. After the performance, gathering outside on the steps of the opera house, it began to snow; it was a dreamlike experience.

Also in the same year there was a wall plaque unveiled to the Venetian erotic poet, Giorgio Baffo. This was conducted in a rather blasphemous way with a 'priest' wearing a penis around his neck instead of a cross, and commedia dell'arte figures dancing. In some ways Baffo was the Venetian equivalent of the Roman poet Giuseppe Belli.

The Venice carnival was already beginning to become commercialised with souvenir shops selling bauta masks and other disguises. In Florence the carnival was mainly an event for children who paraded on the lungarno. The commercialisation in Venice began to rob the event of its mystery as hordes of tourists invaded the city.

11

MARJORIE

My mother came to Gozo several times, and even thought of buying a house there herself. I did not think this was a good idea, she would miss her friends in London, and I was only in Gozo a few months in the year.

However in the late eighties I had a worried telephone call from her neighbour, Maidie Weizmann, to say that Marjorie had had a heart attack, and luckily the postman looked through her letterbox to see her lying on the floor. Maidie got my mother to St Stephen's hospital in the Fulham Road: she had been suffering from hypothermia and was in a bad way. I went to London immediately, staying in her flat and visiting her in the hospital.

She stayed in hospital some weeks, and I came and went to London. the next time I came she was sitting up by her bed, and crying: she was worried about her silver and money which she told me she had put in Switzerland. She told me John Phillips had helped her fly to Basel to sell some jewellery. But her memory was failing, and when I got back to her flat I turned out piles of papers: bills, press cuttings, and letters. I was hoping to find details of an account abroad. I finally found a name scribbled on the back of an envelope, and I took charge of an account with a power of attorney.

I could see that Marjorie would now need full-time care, she had become quite frail, but the nurses told me she could leave hospital. She came back to her flat, and I hired a nurse to stay with her while I went back to Florence to see how I could look after her there. I spoke to Antonio and Grazia who said they would look for a nurse.

But in the meantime Marjorie's accountant had arranged for her to be taken by taxi to a rest home in the country. I got back to London just in time to stop the taxi which was already on its way to London. It turned out that the accountant was a partner in the ownership of the rest home.

Anthony Mathews was very helpful in getting Marjorie to Heathrow where she had a wheelchair for the flight to Pisa. Antonio picked us up and drove us to my flat. Grazia was waiting with a local nurse. Unfortunately though, this nurse could not work full-time as she had her husband to look after. I had to think of something else, and luckily found a young Philippine couple, Franceso and Baby who could live in the flat and look after her full-time. They cooked for her, she liked their Filipino dishes, and took her for a walk every day to a café in Via dei Renai nearby where there was also a small art gallery. Marjorie would talk to people passing by sitting at a table on the pavement outside the café.

Marjorie with Baby at Principina

This arrangement lasted some months and Marjorie seemed quite happy, and was doing some painting as well. She went out to lunch with Sara Kestelman the actress, who was the niece of a friend, and other friends came to visit her.

It was not too easy for me to work in these circumstances, although my flat was so big, and Marjorie was not very enamoured of Florence. I decided that perhaps she would be better off in Gozo with the sunny weather and helpful people. But before taking her there I drove to Barcelona in a second-hand Peugeot 300 with Ilaria, looking for possible homes for her in France on the way. We looked at one or two, but nothing that I felt would be satisfactory.

Eventually I travelled to Gozo with Francesco and Baby. They looked after her well in my house, but after a month or so their permit to stay in Malta ran out, and I had to take them back to Italy, leaving Marjorie in the care of a local family. However on arriving in Rome the Filipinos were not allowed to enter the country as they had not renewed their entry visa to Italy and were left on the other side of the immigration barrier. I knew they had renewed their *permesso di soggiorno* but assumed they had renewed their visa also. This was very sad, as I now could not even approach them, although I was able to pass what money I had on me over to them before they were deported home to the Philippines.

I went back to Gozo and tried to look after Marjorie myself, but it was not really possible: she would fall out of bed, and needed to be washed. I found a local nurse who came daily on a week's trial, but my mother did not take to her, objecting to seeing her eat meat when Marjorie was a vegetarian. After trying to settle her with one of two other families, and looking at rest homes over in Malta, I was having dinner at an Italian restaurant in Marsalforn, the biggest seaside village in Gozo, with my neighbours Hans and Monika, when Hans asked the young waitress if she knew anyone who could care for an old lady. The girl's name was Joyce Frendo and she said her mother who lived in Xaghra, a nearby hill village, could be interested The next week I installed Marjorie in the Calypso hotel in Marsalforn and Joyce's mother Rita, and another lady from Xaghra, Mary Micallef, came down and looked after her every day.

After a month or so a small flat became available in Marsalforn near the sea front. The two ladies thought this would be a better arrangement as they could cook, there was a television, and Marjorie could have a cat and a canary. The owner of the flat who ran a hotel nearby would look in in the evening and early morning to see that all was well. This way I could go back to Florence without worrying, and telephone several times a week to see how things were. At the weekends Joyce would drive my mother to have lunch at a restaurant, or to the hairdresser.

The flat was in a narrow side street and next door lived a woman who would sit outside making lace with a pillow against the wall. My mother would sit next to her and invite passers by to have a look and buy some lace. She also had visitors, Anna Scott and her children, and Jessica, Mary Micallef's daughter came by.

In the spring of 1989 I was in Paris. I had rented a house in the 15th arrondissement, near the Place Denfert-Rochereau from a friend of friends. The telephone rang one afternoon: it was Joyce who told me the doctor had visited Marjorie and her condition was dangerous: she had developed pneumonia, and I should come as soon as possible. I rushed to get to the airport in a taxi and landed at Heathrow only about half-an-hour before the last flight was to take off for Malta. The clerk at the check-in desk was putting away his papers but when I explained about my dying mother in Malta he gave me a boarding card, and as I had no luggage I just made the plane in time, arriving around midnight in Malta.

Marjorie and Joyce at a restaurant in Gozo

Luckily there was ferry during the night and I arrived at Marsalforn in the small hours to find the two ladies with my mother who was comatose in bed. I held her hand and she died early in the morning.

Although her death was to be expected before long it was a great blow to me as we were very close, and being an only child I had very few other close relations left. I arranged for a coffin to be made, and for an Anglican service in the little cemetery chapel in Xewkija, near the centre of Gozo. The English priest had to come by ferry from Malta, and there was a hang-up as the weather was bad and the ferry late. A small congregation of friends was waiting in the churchyard while I went to pick him up in my car and I became worried as he was the last off the boat.

Ann Monsarrat was very helpful to me in the circumstances and arranged for friends to have a drink at Marjorie's flat in Marsalforn. Rita and Mary were very sad and to thank them for all they had done for my mother I helped with a trip to London where they stayed in her flat in the King's Road.

My drawing of Marjorie after death

Back in London I dealt with her probate affairs, and sorted the possessions in her flat, which I kept on. This was not a pleasant task, and a sad one, going through letters, documents and clothes. My mother left the bulk of her estate to me, and there was practically the whole of the contents of Radnor stored in Cranleigh. Brian Catling came down to help me sort some of this out: a lot of furniture that could be sold at auction, together with a great number of paintings of mine and of Majorie's and my grandfather's. I was not going to hurry this too much, but Jamie Maclean knew someone at Bonham's auction house and she came to Rogers in London where the greater part of my grandfather's paintings were stored, and agreed to have a sale of his work in Montpellier street. This went well, and established his work in the market place. Marjorie would have been pleased.

Myself at my mother's grave

She had arranged a show of his watercolours at the Clarges Gallery in Walton Street, London, a few years earlier, but this sale of getting on for one hundred lots put his work on the map.

My father gave me a splendid gold watch for my twenty-first birthday, which had been given to him by Sir Francis on his twenty-first. He asked me to keep it for a future generation, but as I had no children and was unlikely ever to wear it, I decided to sell it at Christie's, where it fetched £6000.

I decided to sell the Madonna by Fungai at Christie's. This sold well to Agnews, and the next year I was surprised to see it exhibited in the 'Mostra dell'Antiqariato' at the Palazzo Strozzi in Florence.

The dealers from Agnews came around to my flat and saw the Sustermans portrait of Ferdinando II de Medici which hung above my desk, and which had been authenticated by a Dutch art historian who happened to be writing a book on Sustermans. I sold this as well in London, and also the Nattier portrait illustrated on page 108.

My father's gold watch

Michèle had left and married Roger Ford, an English writer on military and other matters, and they were now living in a house of a friend of theirs near Prato. For a brief period I rented her room to a Dutch student, Tessa Van der Waals, and after that to an American art historian, Eliot Rowland who was doing a thesis of Filippo Lippi. When he went back to America he worked for Wildenstein in New York, and Georges Wildenstein had mentioned this Nattier portrait (which had previously belonged to the Harland Pecks). Also David Carritt and Wallraf were interested in it. However Christie's got in touch with the author of a catalogue raisonné of Nattier's oeuvre who, without seeing the painting, decided it was 'school of'. This of course affected its price at auction and I was quite disappointed as I was sure the head was Nattier's work.

I was beginning to wonder if I should leave Florence after so many years, and perhaps move to France. On a visit to Paris I was at Geneviève Morgan's flat when a friend of hers stopped by. Her name was Marie Lestringant, and when she knew I might be interested in finding a house for sale took me to visit an acquaintance who was selling her house at Meudon. It was big and interesting, but expensive, and I was not ready to make such a decision. However Marie became a great friend and visited me in Florence. We borrowed Donald Sutphin's old Volkswagen and visited Siena. Later Marie came and stayed in Gozo. She was a dress designer, and has remained a great friend.

Maquette for mural, Gozo (collection Pozzi Florence)

Susan Loewenherz introduced me to an Englishman, Clive Griffiths, who was planning a big exhibition of erotic art, literature, and performance in Bologna. This was to be one of the first shows of its kind, in a big exhibition centre, and it opened in 1992, under the name Erotica 92. Clive had been working in broadcasting and television, and in fact Ilaria Galli appeared in one of his programmes. I had a gallery of my work, as did Susan, and there were long queues to visit the three day event. There were stands selling videos and books, and Jamie Maclean and Tim Hobart had a stand of erotic prints and drawings, with my pop-up book on show. However they sold very little, and several copies of my book were stolen when their back was turned. But the show as a whole was a great success, and was repeated a year or two later under different direction.

In Gozo I had two big projects on the go. One was a mural of the Judgment of Paris in the living room , and the other was the construction of a swimming pool.

Myself and mural 'The Judgment of Paris', Gozo

The mural was to be on the end wall of my living room in Gozo, a space of sixteen feet by nine feet high.

The subject was the Judgment of Paris. I began by modelling the chief actors in the drama, Paris, Hermes, Aphrodite, Athena and Ceres. From the model I made a watercolour drawing. This I squared up onto cartirdge paper the size of the mural, which I fixed to the wall in my studio in Florence. I drew the outlines of the composition, and then cut the drawings into strips which I rolled and took to Gozo.

Meanwhile Joseph Formosa, builder, had prepared the wall which I painted white with emulsion paint. I then transferred my drawing to the wall with carbon paper, and began painting in acrylic colours. I worked on a ladder in a very hot summer, but completed the mural in about a month, and had a grand unveiling by draping a cloth in front of the painting which Ann Monsarrat and Brian Catling then unveiled before twenty or thirty friends whom I had invited.

The reception was good, Aphrodite was likened to a local Gozitan girl by my neighbours in the village, with her black hair. Today the painting has preserved well in spite of the humid climate, and I have not tired of it. It certainly lends another dimension rto the room.

A swimming pool was the other big project in Gozo. On the other side of the small lane that led from the main road to my house there was a patch of land, a field almost, covered with prickly pear, that was being sold by a Gozitan who lived in Australia and was only over on the island for two weeks.

My neighbour Hans and I decided to buy it, and make a large free-form pool, perhaps with an island. But Hans changed his mind, and we carefully divided the plot in two, and he built a studio on his half, and I made the pool on mine.

Construction of swimming pool, Gozo

Many of my friends were undergoing changes in their lives. Hans and Monika, my neighbours in Gozo, separated, although they had never been married. Brian Catling married again, and had two more children, Florence and Finn. Joseph and Ann Rywert were now in Philadelphia where Joseph had a chair of History of Architecture. Anna Scott separated from her husband Robert, and they sold the house in Gozo. Geneviève Morgan divorced her husband Tony, and was now living in rue Saint Antoine, in the Marais. Antonio Masi separated from Maria Grazia and now lived with Jocelyn Fitzgerald who had been a buyer for prestigious shops in London. Ivan Alechine separated from Alexandra who went to live in Brussels.

In London I met a Greek artists, Euphrosyne Doxiadis, at a dinner at Brian Catling's place. She was the daughter of a famous architect and owned a lot of property in Greece. Strangely enough Laurie Preece was her examiner at Wimbledon College of Art. I returned to Florence and we had a passionate correspondence. I returned to London and we had a torrid, if brief, affair. She came to Florence with her son, and we visited Siena, and in London I helped her with a book she was writing on the Fayum portraits. But she had other irons in the fire and our *rapport* did not last.

In Paris I also met an Italian dress designer under strange circumstances.

I was having dinner with Geneviève Morgan and other friends at the Brasserie Balzar, in Saint Germain. I was telling them of the small hotel I was staying at nearby, and I saw a young woman elegantly dressed at the next table dining a lone.

Euphrosyne Doxiadis

I went back to my hotel, and was surpised to receive a phone call an hour or so later. It was the diner at the neighbouring table. She had overheard our conversation and managed to get the hotel concierge to identify me!

We met, and saw each other in Florence and in London. Her name was Ersilia Gargioli and she lived in Milan, but had rented an office in Paris where she hoped to break into one of the big couture houses. In fact, she was already selling her desgins at chic stores in Paris.

Later Ersilia was instrumental in my meeting my future wife Chantal, but more of that later. In 1990 I stayed a night with Ersilia in Milan on my way to the great Velasquez exhibition in Madrid. I had the foresight to take my shooting stick as the queue was about four hours long, and I was the envy of the other queuers. In Madrid I met a young friend of Michèle's who invited me to tapas and a nightspot with two other girls. She left me to get a taxi after midnight, but there were none, I was completely lost, but was amazed to find that the metro was still running, and I got back safely to my hotel.

I did not find Madrid a beautiful city, although the Prado was overwhelming and the Tiepolo ceilings in the Royal Palace were spectacular. I also saw Picasso's Guernica at the Cason del Buen Retiro. I noticed that nobody gave a glance to the splendid ceiling of Luca Giordano, which, if the Picasso had not been there, should have elicited great praise.

In 1991 I went to Konstanz for Hans Dörflinger's fiftieth birthday, a big reception with cabaret acts and songs. At the hotel I was staying at I was waiting for Hans to arrive, but another woman was also waiting and we struck up conversation. Her name was Ingrid Maegle, and she was an art dealer with her base in the small village of Wiecks, not far away. She later came to Gozo, and helped me promote my work. A friend of hers printed a series of cards with reproductions of my paintings tipped in, and these were held in black boxes which a box maker in Florence produced. We went to a gallery in Munich whioch Richard Fremantle recommended as they had had a show of a friend of his, but apart from visiting the Munich Erotic Art Museum, and Neuschwanstein, King Ludwig's castle, nothing came of the visit.

Later on I called Karl Ludwig Leonhardt, the great collector of erotica in Hamburg: I had spoken to him before about 'Sophie's Dream Book.' He told me about the Erotic Art Museum in Hamburg, the collection of which was largely based on his loans, and I went to Hamburg with Ingrid who had become a close friend, and we met Karl Ludwig and his wife Sieglinde. He introduced me to Claus Becker, the director of the museum, and we discussed

David Russell   A Midsummer Night's Dream   150 x 250 cm   1984

the possibility of a show. The Museum had not long been open, in the St.Pauli district, not far from the notorious Reeperbahn. It was housed in what had been a warehouse on three floors, and provided a splendid space for exhibiting. At that moment there was a show of the graphic artist Topor and upstairs were Karl Luwig's loans.

In principle, with Leonhardt's blessing, Becker was prepared to give me a show, and later in the year he and his wife came to Florence to see my studio. They stayed at the Albergo Berchielli, and then the Porta Rossa. We ate out at a simple restaurant, and they liked my work, not only the erotic paintings, but also the earlier geometrical ones. Later Karl Ludwig also came with his wife, on their way south.

I began doing paintings for the show, and ordered some large canvasses. The exhibition was to be in 1995, so I had time to do a number of works. There was a lot of space to fill.

The paintings were explicitly erotic, with mythological overtones, Cupid as well as Ganesh. I did small drawings which I squared up to the canvas. I found an excellent framer in Borgo Santo Spirito, and had mostly gilt frames made, which Becker paid for.

In the meantime Ingrid and I took some trips: to Egypt in 1992, and later to Tenerife.

Egypt was all I hoped for. We flew to Luxor, changing planes in Cairo, and stayed at the Mövenpick hotel which biordered the Nile, and had a botanical garden and zoo, and a platform to view the sunset across the river.

We took a felucca across the river to the valley of the Kings, and hired a taxi on the other side, and explored tombs and saw the great sphinx. A copt taxi driver also took us to see sites near Luxor, and we went to a *Son et Lumière* performance at the temple of Karnak.

Ingrid with Colossus of Memnon

We never got as far as Aswan, but the atmosphere of the temples in Luxor and Thebes made a great impression on me, as did the temple of Hathor at Denderah, with its relief sculptures, lit by slanting sunlight when we were there.

We went on for another week to Cairo, and stayed at another Mövenpick hotel at Giza. We went to the pyramids, had photos on camelback, and I ventured inside the great Cheops pyramid, frightenly claustrophobic. We also went to Coptic churches and of course the Cairo Museum and the relics of Tutankhamen, so splendid in contrast to the old-fashioned cases with their hand-written labels. It was also interesting to see the Fayum portraits, which Euphrosyne was preparing a book about.

Another trip abroad with Ingrid took us to Tenerife. Ingrid had a temporary job at a German hotel in the north of the island. She met me at the airport, and I had the strange experience of staying in a totally German hotel, akin to my experience in Taormina staying at a Danish hotel. Ingrid had her own office, and there were walks in the surrounding hills, as well as by the sea. We rented a car and saw something of the island, especially the botanic gardens in Puerto de la Cruz which date from the eighteenth century, and contain plants that grew in my Gozo garden.

After a week in the German hotel Ingrid found a small flat to rent in Santa Cruz. It belonged to a German psychologist, Heidi Fittkau-Garthe, who was the 'earth mother' of a religious cult on the island. There was later a scandal of mass suicide of the members, which was averted in time. Santa Cruz, the capital of Tenerife, was a rather down-at-heel town, a relic of better days, it seemd. There was an art museum with some work of Dominguez who had been an acquaintance of Edward Wright, and was a native of Tenerife.

Ingrid and I also drove around the Italian lakes, visiting once again the Villa Taranto, and Cannero where my father had thought of buying a house many years before. At Christmas Ingrid invited Brian Catling and his new wife and children to stay in Wiecks. After two days of staying in Ingrid's flat, she found them a sort of hotel-cum-zoo nearby, that is to say a hotel with animals: horses, wild boar, birds: ideal for children to play.

A commission came from a friend of Michèle, Andrea Godi. He wanted a large painting of a scene with his two sons. He left the subject to me, but I invented a classical fantasy with nymphs, Silenus, and the façade of Santo Spirito, as well as various Palladian buildings. I painted this in Gozo, and as usual rolled it in a cardboard tube to take to Italy.

Bruce Winston and his new wife Barbara visited me in Gozo, and I gave a party for them, inviting friends including Ann Monsarrat and others of the 'English colony' as it were.

There was quite a social life on the island, but especially of expatriates from England, and a few from Germany and Scandinavia. In the early nineties property was still cheap, and the facility of the Maltese for their secind language, English, was a great attraction to many.

Barbara and Bruce Winston, and Ann Monsarrat

On another occasion Bruce invited me to the Monaco Grand Prix. I was to join him at his hotel, stay the night and see the race the next day. I took the train from Florence, quite a tiresome journey, arriving in the morning. Bruce had told me he would be either at the Hotel de Paris, or Loews. I asked at both hotels, but no indication of a reservation. I said tto the concierge at Loews 'Surely you know Mr. Winston, the son of Harry Winston?' He said 'Is he connected?' I replied 'I don't think so!' Anyway he let me leave my suitcase in the hotel, and I went to see the Jardins Botaniques up the hill.

In the afternoon I asked again, but no booking at either hotel. In the end I sat in the garden in front of the Casino reading the Daily Telegraph and wondering what to do. I knew all the small hotels would be booked up, and if I did not find Bruce I would have to go to Menton or somewhere else for the night.

I looked up from my newspaper, and there was Bruce strolling through the garden. I was really happy to see him. It turned out that he had booked both at the Hotel de Paris and Loews, but in his agent's name, forgetting to tell me. We stayed at Loews, had dinner at the Hotel de Paris, and watched the race: too close to the cars to even identify them as they sped past. But I could see how thrilled the fans were, though it did very little for me.

I also saw Annalita again in France. As I said before she had inherited a château near Brie, and I went to visit her. She had a stable block in the grounds and offered it to me to rent, but it would have needed a great deal of alteration to live in. But the little château was beautiful. She told me more about her mother, how Marlys wanted to take an injunction of alienation of affection against her husband Clay (whom she had now divorced.) Annalita made an contract with her that she could have the apartment in Park Avenue if she agreed never to see her daughter again.

David Russell Marchesa Marsigli 1960

I had now to concentrate on the show in Hamburg, and do a lot of work. Around this time I had another problem: Sebastiano, the son of Count Capponi, wanted to bring an end to the lease of my flat. He came to look at it with his fiancée, saying that they would like to live in my flat, and that perhaps he could find me somewhere else to live in Florence. I later found out that he had said the same thing to other tenants of 28 Via de' Bardi. Fortunately I had an excellent woman lawyer, a very militant Calabrese, and for the time she kept the landlord at bay. But a decision was needed.

Spring

Summer

David Russell: Ilaria Galli in the four seasons

Autumn

Winter

My Parents in Torquay

Marjorie and cat, Marsalforn

Marjorie and Ann Monsarrat

Marjorie in my garden, Gozo

Marjorie Russell Cyclamen, oil on paper 1981

Marjorie and Sara Kestelman, Floremce

12

HAMBURG AND PARIS

The date for the Hamburg exhibition was now March 1995. I had another trip with Ingrid to see Claus Becker about details of the catalogue and transport and framing of the paintings. We agreed in principle, though Becker was not always the easiest person to deal with. The catalogue was to be printed in Spain in English, German and French, but in the event I was not able to read the proofs and there were many mistakes.

Brian Catling agreed to come to the *vernissage* of the show, and make a speech, also Kathleen Michael, now living in Germany, would dance. Other friends who came for the opening were Laurie Preece and Susan Lowenherz, as well as Ivan Alechine on his way to Brussels.

Brian made a reasoned introduction to my work in English, but it seemed to be well understood by the visitors and press. One of the patrons of the Erotic Museum in Copenhagen bought a painting, and two other geometrical works were sold. Karl Ludwig Leonhardt also bought two paintings.

Brian Catling, Kathleen Michael and myself, Hamburg

One was 'The Garden of Women', and the other 'Saint Teresa' (illustrated on page 124.) The 'Garden of Women' Karl Ludwig hung above his desk in his Hamburg apartment on Heinrich Hertz Strasse, and the other in his house in Schleswig Holstein. Both places were full of books and paintings: in Hamburg he had a bookcase with all the books in Perceau's bibliography.

I stayed with the Leonhardts in their country house, in a room full of books of course, and we watched 'The Maltese Falcon' after dinner on television, but in German. Fortunately I knew the film well and was not too bored at not understanding the dialogue.

Karl Ludwig and Sieglinde Leonhardt

It was of course fascinating to talk to Karl Ludwig about erotica. He had such a wide knowledge of all aspects of the subject, and corresponded with Patrick Kearney who was an admirer of 'Sophie's Dream Book', and Cliff Scheiner the eccentric book dealer whom I had met in New York: an old friend of Edie Solow. He gave me a copy of 'The Private Case', the bibliography by Patrick Kearney of the British Museum collection of erotica.

Back in Florence I had now to deal with the possibility of giving up my splendid apartment. My *avvocatessa* Josefina Froyo assured me that I could stay on at least another four years, and the 'so-called Count Capponi' could no nothing about it. But somehoew I did not want to live under the cloud of an eviction at a later date.

In fact Sebastiano Capponi showed me one or two other flats to which I could move, one of which was a splendid place in the Palazzo Torrigiani, quite nearby, and overlooking the river Arno and Via Renai. I thought long and hard about this. The Contessa Torrigiani was charming and without doubt would be a good landlady, but after much reflection I decided that I did not want to spend the rest of my life in Florence, seductive as the city was, and I decided to have a look in Paris where I still had a number of good friends, and which I thought would be a stimulating place to live. It was a very difficult decision.

I went to Paris and Marie Lestringant again helped me look for a flat to rent. I looked at one on the Ile St.Louis, but it would have been too small to house all my paintings, furniture and books. That was obviously going to be the problem, unless I could also afford a separate studio.

Eventually with Marie's help I found a possible flat. It was in the rue Beaubourg, near the Pompidou Centre and not far from Marks and Spencer's store!

Although the monthly rent was a good deal more than what I was paying in Florence (where the rent was still subject to the *equo canone,*) I calculated that I could house most of my furniture and books, and there would be two bedrooms and a room I could use as a studio. I drew a plan, and when Grazia Zatti was in Paris she helped measure the spaces. I agreed to a *bail*, and contacted Gondrand the shippers to give me an estimate for moving to Paris, furniture and books. Sebastiano Capponi agreed to pay my moving costs. I left a fine eighteenth century clothes press in the flat, also a big red carpet which had been in the 'red room' at Radnor. I left also my big brass bed which I remembered in Sir Francis's room at Lewes Crescent in Brighton. These were all too big to take to Paris. However I bought a four-poster bed in Florence and included that in the removals.

The flat in rue Beaubourg was on the fifth floor of a Haussman type building, with a Portuguese concierge and a lift. It also had a small balcony and two rooms looked on to a courtyard at the back. There was a good restaurant nearby, 'Le Hangar', and good shopping in rue Rambuteau.

The Italian removal men from Gondrand hired a telescopic platform to lift my possessions from the street to the fifth floor through a window, and I anxiously awaited the objects to arrive one by one. I had packed the books myself. I had sold about one hundred children's books of mine a month or two previously, which I later regretted: Rupert the Bear annuals, Tiger Tim, Mary Plain, Chick's Own, Winnie the Pooh. But I kept the rest of the books which now amounted to nearly 3000. I used one wall of the living room to house them, and by cutting out the sizes of pieces of furniture to scale in paper, I managed to place everything before I left Florence. Even the marble copy of a Canova statue, Venus and Adonis from Geneva. Incidentally I had been

Marie Lestringant

on a trip by car to Venice with Ilaria, and we had visited Canova's incredible studio at Possagno, which Salvador Dali had told me about years before. My statue somehow fitted in a corner of the living room with my spinet.

Marie helped me arrange the rooms, and made curtains for the four-poster, and seat covers for the dining chairs. The kitchen was small but adequate, with a service staircase.

I should have mentioned one or two other events which happened before leaving Florence. One was appearing in the James Ivory film 'A Room with a View.' I only had a part as an extra, especially in the scene at Santa Croce, but the experience was fascinating. Each day I would put on my costume, the costumier being nearby in Via San Niccolò, and turn up for the shoot. My screen wife was Jane Moorman, an American living in Florence, and my screen daughter was a young girl, another Ilaria. I prompted Denholm Eliot who had forgotten his lines in the church, and had a scene crossing the Piazza della Signoria. Ivory was a great perfectionist and shot the scenes often ten or twenty times. I also appeared in another film shot near Siena in which John Gielgud appeared, 'War and Remembrance,' from the Herman Wouk novel.

Myself and Jane Moorman in 'A Room with a View'.

Another project before leaving Florence was a series of nine etchings printed by Vittoria Pozzi, and representing the transformations of Zeus as lover. Ilaria Galli wrote a preface to this volume which was launched at the shop of Franco Maria Ricci. In all these endeavours the advice of Anthony Mathews was invaluable. He was now working for Scala Editrice, the important fine art publishers and archivists in Florence, and he bought a farmhouse in Fiesole where he lived with his wife June and family, before moving to Oxford.

I was of course going to miss all my friends in Florence, the madrigal evenings, the *trattorie*, the Sunday outings with Antonio Masi and Joss to the countryside. Also the Italian culture: the cinema, the exhibitions, the theatre and opera. But then Paris had its compensations: a big city again, like my native London, and a closer hop to the flat in Chelsea, via the new Eurostar train. This was a considerable bonus.

A year or two before moving I had been at a party, a boîte in fact, with Ersilia Gargioli, and I met a girl who was dancing and whom I felt very attracted to. I managed to get her telephone number, and called the next day. Her name was Chantal Thomas and I invited her for a drink at 'La Coupole', and dinner round the corner

Anthony Mathews

at 'La Closerie des Lilas.'

The evening went well, and when back in Florence I sent her a copy of my book 'Sophie.' When I went to live in Paris I tried calling her number, but the line was disconnected. I went to her address in the 17e arrondissement but there was no response to her bell, and I left a message for the concierge with my phone number. Fortunately Chantal went to pick up her mail and found my note: she had moved to a flat in Levallois, and I made contact again.

From then on we saw a lot of each other. Chantal came to Gozo, and to London. I painted her portrait in Gozo, and in London we had dinner at the Savile Club, and took a short trip to Jersey.

My mother's flat was very useful.

Chantal in rue Beaubourg

I had been going to the 'Sex Maniac's Ball', an event organised by Tuppy Owens who lived in Mayfair and who ran a charity devoted to helping disabled people with sex problems, and communication. It was a strange and rather English event, perhaps not quite as erotic as one could have hoped. This particular year Chantal and I rented costumes in Paris, and took a taxi to the venue which this year was in Brixton, from the King's Road.

Unfortunately though when we banged on the door of the club where the ball was to take place, there was no response. Stuck in a seedy neighbourhood in our costumes we began to be worried: there was no sign of a taxi or bus. The only hope was for some other benighted people to turn up in a car, which eventually happened, and we got a lift back to Sloane Square. The next morning there was to be a protest led by Tuppy in Piccadilly Circus, attended by Cicciolina, the Hungarian porno star and deputy in the Italian parliament. But again we unfortunately missed her. The reason for the cancellation of the ball was a police enquiry which had never happened before, and of course Tuppy was furious at losing money for her charity.

We went to Oxford and stayed with Brian Catling and his wife Sarah who was planning a book on anatomy for artists, later to be published with great success. We also used to have breakfast with Anna Scott at the Picasso café in the King's Road.

Further along the King's Road, at number 356, a friend from Gozo, a painter, opened a small art gallery and asked me to exhibit.

I was very happy to do so, and brought quite a number of paintings from Hamburg. I shared the gallery with a friend, Monica Guevara, who also did erotic drawings and had worked with Jamie Maclean.

The show got off to a good start with a big 'vernissage', however Kim was not an experienced art dealer, and after the opening, as often happens, there were not a great many visitors, apart from friends, in spite of its good location. The gallery did not last long, and I think became a bar.

Myself, Carole Smith, and my cousin Peter at the opening of the show.

Laurie Preece helped me retrieve a lot of my paintings from Mann's in Cranleigh. One or two had been damaged and they had to pay for restoration through their insurance company. But a much more serious loss happened at their warehouse. I had asked an antique dealer and restorer, a friend of Jamie Maclean, to come and look at items I wanted to sell: there were some superb French clocks from Radnor, and other items that I would never be able to house, and I agreed that for a small fee this dealer would sell these objects at Christies South Kensington, sending me the catalogues. Which he did. However we put aside certain pieces of furniture including a fine French cabriole table, which I planned to keep. The next time I went down to Mann's warehouse about a dozen of these pieces of furniture had disappeared.

There had been a new warehouse manager, a man who had recently retired from another job, and he was obviously not conscious enough of security. I aslo had my suspicious of the antique dealer, but of course no proof whatever.

As with the theft from Radnor a few years before, I fortunately had photographs of the stolen items, but as before certainly did not receive their full value from the insurance company.

Some of my paintings, early ones on masonite that I left with Laurie, I destroyed, and the others were sent back to Tandem in Frechen-bei-Köln.

A year or so before I left for Paris I was in Gozo where Laurie and his wife Jane were staying with me. I was doing my shopping in Victoria, the capital of Gozo, when climbing a hill I suddenly felt severely out of breath. I went to the central polyclinic where a doctor examined me. He told me to go immediately to the hospital as I had a heart problem. At the hospital they wanted to keep me, and if I left, to sign a form of exculpation for them. I understood the gravity of the situation, but went home to talk to Laurie and Jane, and then returned to the hospital where I was seen by the heart specialist, Dr Farrugia.

It turned out to be quite a serious condition and I was kept in the coronary unit for ten days or so. My heart was monitored day and night, and I had a medication which resulted in atrial fibrillation. I felt somewhat weak and tired, and though the Gozo hospital treatment was excellent, the food was not...many friends came and visited me bringing titbits to eat!

Laurie and Jane were most helpful, and stayed on longer to help me when I got out of hospital. Linda Lloyd Jones had travelled back from India recently, and sitting next to her on the plane was a heart surgeon whom she got to know: by coincidence he worked from time to time in Malta. His name was David Brennand Roper and had trained Doctor Farrugia. I went to see him in London at the London Bridge Hospital, and have seen him every year since then.

In Florence Doctor Mario Nepi gave me advice, and recommended a cardiologist there whom I also visited. Mario became a great friend. He and his wife Mimmi had a splendid villa in via Santa Margherita dei Montici, and he bought a painting which hung in the vast salone, illustrated here.

David Russell 'Three Women' collection Nepi

Back in Paris I was seeing a lot of Chantal, going to clubs, excursions at the weekends to places around Paris: Vaux le Vicomte, Auvers-sur-Oise and the cemetery where Van Gogh was buried, the sale of the country house of Charles de Beistegui at Groussay, 'France Miniature' at Elancourt, and the guinguette at Nogent-sur-Seine.

A friend, the dress designer Ersilia Gargioli came to stay from Italy as she was looking for a position in a couture house, and Brian came from London, and Laurie and Jane. I saw a lot of Geneviève Morgan now living in rue Saint Antoine, and I painted a portrait of her daughter Charlotte when about twelve years old.

I began painting in one of the rooms of the flat, but I was strapped for space. Chantal's brother Franck constructed a framework to stack my paintings, but before long I decided with Chantal's help to look for a studio.

We had a look in the Filles de Calvaire area in the eleventh arrondissement, and Chantal asked around in various courtyards where there were many artisans' workshops and studios. In rue Oberkampf, nosing around in a courtyard, Chantal found an ideal place: a lop-sided door led into a working space next to a potter and a jewellery designer. It was twenty minutes' walk from rue Beaubourg, and I could rent it by the month at a reasonable rate. I

Corridor, 28 rue Beaubourg

could walk there in twenty minutes, via rue Vieille du Temple.

Franck helped again building a sort of mezzanine to store paintings. I would go most days, principally working on sculptures in clay, which the potter next door would fire for me. Some of these sculptures I cast in bronze at a factory in the south of France.

In Paris there was a new 'Musée de l'Erotisme' and I went along with photographs of my work, and the catalogue from Hamburg. It turned out that they knew Claus Becker well and that he was keen on a tie-up between the two museums.

The museum was situated on the Boulevard Clichy near sex shops and 'live shows', but the museum was well organised on seven floors, and had a remarkable permanent collection of artefacts , paintings and sculptures from around the world. They agreed to give me a show of my paintings and sculpture, but I shared the space with another painter (the story of my life!)

Many friends came to the *vernissage,* but as usual not much was sold. The larger paintings went back to Tandem after the show. The museum had some good shows and unusually was open until the small hours of the night.

After that show I did not make a great effort to find a gallery in Paris. My work was now changing: I was reintroducing geometrical elements into the compositions, as well as using the Camera Lucida again after many years .

Chantal and I made a trip to Scotland, staying first at the New Club in Edinburgh and seeing the sights there, and then visiting my cousin Agnes in Perth, and Neto and Tom Hunter in Kirriemuir, and then west to Fort William where we stayed at Inverlochy Castle in a very luxurious setting. Then the ferry to Skye where we had bad weather and could hardly see the 'far Coulins'!

We made another trip to Scotland when we were in Gozo and heard that my cousin Neto had died of pancreatic cancer. I decided to go to the funeral and got a flight to London, and to Dundee from the City airport.

We stayed with Neto's daughter Susan, and her husband John Mountford in Kirriemuir. It was a sad occasion, and I now only had one first cousin left, Agnes Moncrieff. Tommy was heartbroken, and a lot of his relations came to the funeral from another part of Scotland.

Chantal and I also took a nostalgic trip to Florence, staying at the Hotel Porta Rossa where I had stayed many years before. I introduced Chantal to Ilaria, to Joss and Antonio, and to Don and Caroline Sutphin. We went up to Don's studio in Erta Canina, and had lunch in via San Niccolò. We went to Fiesole and saw via de' Bardi where I had lived for so long.

Back in Paris we visited Chantal's family on the Côtes- d'Armor in Brittany.

Chantal was born at Chartres, but her parents were now back near Guingamp, as were four of her brothers. The fifth, Franck, lived in the 77, Seine-et Marne, district, not far from Paris.

Her other brothers were Alain, Serge, Christian and Jean-Claude and her only sister Dany. Her father had been a farmer, having moved to Normandy at one stage, and was now retired. Very sadly he died a year or two after I met him.

We borrowed a car from Serge and did a trip along the coast, visiting some islands, one with thousands of sea birds. We did not get very far: I would have liked, and

Chantal and Don Sutphin at his studio

I hope still will one day, visit Finisterre and the Belle Île, also the forest of Brocéliand.

The Bretons go in for sumptuous and long parties, especially for weddings and baptisms. I found these difficult to survive, apart from the language problem. My French was getting better, however communication was not always easy especially when talking fast. Later we also visited Dany and her husband Franck who were living in Perigueux. They took us to visit the caves at Lascaux, and Bergerac and other places in the Dordogne.

Chantal's brother Jean-Claude lived in a village to the west of Guingamp where he had an important business making the compost for growing mushrooms, as well as the mushrooms themselves. He had expanded into Poland

Chantal in Brittany

and Italy, as well as Canada, and had a thriving business, helped by his brother Christian. He collected old cars, and had two daughters. He had been blinded in one eye, but this did not hinder his exhuberant character.

All Chantal's brothers are very successful in their different ways, Alain and Franck being *ébenistes*, and Serge working in real estate.

Chantal's parents lived in a small village called Pabu, and after the death of Chantal's father, her mother Huguette continues to live there, near to four of her sons.

They have all been very welcoming to me, and I felt something in common with their Celtic spirit. They have great family solidarity, but at the same time great independence. Chantal had left Brittany quite early in her life, and studied gemology in Paris, and opened an antique jewellery shop near Saint Lazare with a partner. There she had at least one lucky escape when a thief drew a revolver: Chantal managed to knock it out of his hand, but still has a scar where she was cut.

Christian, Dany, Franck, Serge, Jean-Claude, Alain and Chantal Thomas

In February 1997 Chantal and I took a trip to Thailand. This was partly the result of my old friend John Phillips having settled in Phuket, after Roquebrune and Vevey. He had a suite in a hotel, the Allamanda, near the sea, and was not planning to return to Europe.

We took the flight to Bangkok and stayed a night or two at the Shangri-La Hotel, and visited Jim Thomson's house, a tour on the canals, and Queen Sirikit's botanical gardens.

We decided to fly north to Chiang Mai, and explore the north of the country. We stayed in a 'bed and breakfast', and met an Englishman who had just published a guide to the region. We went out to dinner with him and his Thai wife, and he told us of someone with a jeep who could take us exploring the north for a few days.

We duly set off with the driver/guide, and went towards the Mekong river and border with Burma. We stopped at a Chinese village, and another one where the women had their necks stretched with a series of rings added gradually. We took photographs, but found that these girls were exploited, and originally came from Burma.

We also visited a village in the wilds where supposedly they had never seen strangers or a car. Lastly we took a boat ride down the Mekong, with Laos on the far side, and after an hour or two our driver picked us up, and we made

Chantal and myself on elephant back

our way back to Chiang Mai. It had been fascinating, a very new experience for me who had never been in the East, seeing the rice paddies, riding on a very temperamental elephant, and eating delicious food.

Our next destination was Phuket where we were to stay in the hotel Allamanda where my old friend John Phillips was now living.

The hotel was on a lagoon near the coast, one of several hotels and a shopping centre which were reached by a small ferry boat.

There were excellent restaurants in the hotels of different nationalities, but the best food was at small bistros on the beach nearby. Superb prawns, and local dishes, and fresh pine-

Chantal in a rice paddy

apples. John had settled into his suite, having sold a lot of his possessions when leaving Switzerland, and now seemed very happy with an easy-going new life.

We made our own excursions with a taxi driver in Phuket: to a park where Gibbons were being raised, in the jungle, and a hotel in Phuket itself.

Chantal had a Thai massage, and was given a drink which left her, for a moment, in a hallucinatory state. We found the Thais charming, and very helpful, apart from the tuk-tuk taxi drivers who insisted on going to shops where they had a rake-off. But that does not only happen in Thailand.

Myself with elephant sculpture, Phuket

Back in Paris I had several visitors to rue Beaubourg, for one Margaret my ex-wife who was now working in psychiatry with the American army in Germany, also Brian Catling who had a small exhibition at the Galerie Satellite in Paris. Laurie also came over for a party at the British Embassy for the sculptor Bill Pye, and Sarah and Kildare Burke-Borrowes who were looking for a pied-à-terre in Paris.

Our next visit was to Florida. The way it came about was that whenI was in Florence, Hans Dörflinger proposed that I exchange my flat with a friend, Alice Bellony who had a big studio flat near St.Paul in Paris. This worked out well, and she proposed that we join her and her sister and niece in a holiday home on a golf course near Orlando.

Neither Chantal nor I had been to Florida, and as it was cold in Paris it seemed like a good idea. We flew to Orlando and rented a car at the airport and drove to the house near Clermont, to the west.

Our relations with Alice's niece did not work out well. Fortunately we had a separate entrance to the house, but she had a rude and obstreperous child and she was rude and obstreperous herself. After visiting the amazing Disneyland and Epcot and going boating on a lake with Alice, we decided to set off in our rented car to see the rest of Florida.

We cut across to Tampa and down the west coast, staying at St. Petersburg, and Sarasota, and the Gasparilla Inn at Boca Grande, recommended by our friend Suzy Patterson, and supposedly frequented by the Bush family.

There we had a sort of small cottage, and a meal in the main hotel: somewhat pretentious! For me perhaps the most interesting part of our journey were the museums: the Edison (and Ford) house at Fort Myers, and the Ringling Museum at Sarasota, as well as the interesting collection of ancient

Greek art at Tampa. Moving on we crossed Florida on the Tamiami trail, stopping on the way at an American Indian restaurant, and taking a sort of train to see the alligators and other wild life.

We decided to go down the Keys, and spent a night at Key Largo, and another at Key West, having seen round Hemingway's house.

Going back to the mainland we stopped at a wonderful botanic garden, the Fairchild Tropical Gardens. I had never seen such splendid gardens with their different zones, the rainforest, the enormous collection of palms. You could go round in a buggy:, by lagoons. We

Chantal at Vizcaya Villa, Miami-Dade

also visited Villa Vizcaya, an incredible reproduction of a Venetian villa, with antique Venetian furniture, and a splendid formal garden. It was built by James Deering, a farm machinery tycoon, and he spent the winters there from 1916 to 1925. Now a public museum it has an extraordinary atmosphere, and the attention to detail is such that you can really believe yourself in the Veneto. These two visits were worth the whole trip for me: the villa was luckily discovered by Chantal.

We went further north, and at Coconut Grove we arranged to meet our friend from Italy, Susan Loewenherz, who was staying there with her brother. Negotiating the incredible spaghetti-like freeway into Miami itself, I managed to end up on South Beach and book in at an art deco hotel which had seen better times, but which was central, and we were able to people-gaze on the sidewalk by the sea.

The next day we headed north again in the direction of Cape Canaveral which we saw in the distance before cutting across to Orlando and back to the golf course and Alice. It had been an exhausting but fascinating drive in a car with automatic gears which I had never driven before.

Chantal and Susan Loewenherz

In Paris we were having some trouble with my landlord, a Monsieur Joyeux, an inappropriate name if ever there was. He insisted that my flat was a second home as I was resident in Malta, and therefore he could put up the rent when it pleased him. For twenty years now I had been living in rented accommodation, and both Chantal and I thought that it was perhaps time to buy a place to live. Chantal had her own very nice flat in Levallois Neuilly, but if we could find a big place in the centre with room for a studio, she would sell her place, and we would share the costs of a new apartment.

We started looking, preferably in the same area as rue Beaubourg, and contacted several agents. After quite a lot of fruitless search we visited a property in rue d'Anjou, near the Madeleine, in the 8th arrondissement.

We approached the building from the north, little realising in fact that it was very near the Faubourg Saint Honoré, and the British Embassy. It was on the second floor, more than 200 square meters in size, with three huge reception rooms with ornate stucco ceilings and marble fireplaces, as well as two other smaller rooms, kitchen and antiquated bathroom.

We had not seen anything like it, at its price. It had just been advertised, and Chantal was on the doostep of the agent's office when it opened at 9 on the Monday following the visit. The telephone was ringing with offers, but by negotiating well, Chantal's offer was accepted. She also sold her flat well, I transferred some money from Basel, and we began the process of moving house once again.

As usual moving was quite traumatic, but there was no shortage of space now to put all my furniture, and Chantal's, and books and paintings.

There were several conveniences of the flat: a lift, a concierge, a coded entrance, a courtyard, and the central location. The whole building had belonged to a Jewish family, the Kriegs, and they still occupied three of the nine or so apartments in the building. Two were spinsters who did their shopping round the corner at Franprix, and a brother who lived on the same floor opposite us. We bought the flat from another brother who was an amateur pianist, and he sold us one

Entrance Hall, 7 rue d'Anjou, Paris

of his pianos, an old Érard, but still serviceable. (I had sold my Steinberg to a friend before leaving Italy.) We moved in, in 1998.

Chantal, her Mother, Nolwen, Doriane, Dany, her Father

Chantal, rue Beaubourg

Chantal, Gozo

Karine with Nolwen and Doriane, Franck and Chantal, rue Beaubourg

Myself and Chantal at a restaurant

Chantal and 'Statue', Barcelona

My seventieth birthday at Le Pré Catalan

Chantal at 'France Miniature'

David Russell Chantal in Gozo, oil on canvas 1998

Chantal at Vizcaya, Florida

13

MARRIAGE IN GOZO

It was, of course, wonderful to have so much space.Chantal had her room, I had the big studio for which Franck built racks for paintings, and big cupboards for clothes. The entrance hall housed most of my books, a dining table of Chantal's, and the piano from M.Krieg.

Jimmy, a Filipino who had come to rue Beaubourg to clean and tidy, now came to the new flat. He was now married (we went to a splendid wedding reception,) and had a little girl. I arranged for the cable television, and used the minitel, a small computer given in France alongside the telephone, and a sort of introduction to a real computer.

In fact a year or so later I decided to plunge into the world of computing. My friend Roger Ford said I would kick myself for the years I had not done so, and so it turned out. I bought a computer from an English firm which delivered to France, with an English keyboard. A PC with Windows XP, which I still use. It opened an amazing world of information. I could catalogue my 3000 books; I could write professional letters. A great discovery.

We spent quite a lot of time at the flat in the King's Road in London, although the maintenance costs were getting expensive. Some friends from Gozo, Sonja and George Sinclair Stevenson stayed a while in the flat and talked about buying it. Then George died, and Sonja became even more persistent about her desire to have the flat as a pied-à-terre in London. Eventually I gave in, with a contract that I could stay in the flat for six weeks every year, at times agreeable to both. For a while this worked out well, but after a couple of years Sonja decided she wanted to be free to come to London when she wanted, and proposed paying off our agreement.

I consulted my solicitor and although he had drawn up a contract, it would be void if she sold or gave away the flat. For example she could give it to her son, and still use it.

She proposed a very inadequate sum in compensation, about one quarter of its long term value. Looking back I foolishly accepted a small sum, and reluctantly said goodbye to my mother's flat, and the possibility of long stays in London. But in a way it was a relief, as Sonja had been extremely difficult about our staying there, not even allowing me to keep a toaster in the little kitchen. Added to which she had redone the apartment in bad taste, and the memories of it when my mother lived there were obliterated.

Rue d'Anjou did not perhaps turn out to be the liberating place we thought it to be. Chantal was taking English lessons at the British Institute and progressing really well, but my painting somewhat fell in the doldrums, and I was not as energetic about finding galleries and shows as I should have been.

Salon, rue d'Anjou

However we had some good dinner parties, and even a dinner party with a piano recital by a young pianist on the Érard. For Christmas we had been to Gozo, but now had a party here with a tree bought at the *marché* by the Madeleine. After two Christmases in Gozo we decided to visit other places, and the first of these was Barcelona.

It was the year of the Millenium, and for new year's eve we were invited to a party at a friend of Geneviève Morgan, in the rue des Augustins on the left bank. We drank to the new year at midnight, and then went onto the Pont Neuf to see the fireworks, and the Eiffel Tower lit up. When younger I had never expected to survive to the new millenium, but here I was with Chantal, happy and looking forward to the future.

We decided to get married later that year in Gozo. It was partly a practical matter as I was resident there, and we set the date for the 14th October. Chantal invited her sister Dany as 'maid of honour', and I invited my friend Gigi Dimech as my best man.

It was a nice day in October, the 14th., and I wore a grey silk suit I had bought in London. We had some breakfast at a café in Victoria, and walked over to the Registry Office, which had a small courtyard where the ceremony was to take place. We saw a figure walking towards us in the street wearing dark glasses and in the distance looking like a Mafia boss. It was Brian Catling who had arrived as a surprise with a bunch of flowers.

Gigi who was my witness, and his wife Joyce, and Chantal's sister Dany assembled in the courtyard and signed the various necessary documents. The ceremony was over quite quickly, and we went home to prepare for a reception in our house that evening.

Chantal decided she would do the cooking, an Indian meal, and we hired two elderly waiters to pass dishes around. There were 40 or so guests, mainly expatriate English, but also some Maltese friends. Brian stayed with Ann Monsarrat, and we saw him again the next day

We went to Valletta to register the marriage at the French Embassy, and there were other procedures to go through when we got back to France.

Louis Dimech, Chantal, Myself, Dany, Joyce Dimech
Children: Stefan, Larissa and Yana Dimech

Life did not seem so different, but I hoped our union was more secure. I was resident in Gozo after all, and I hoped this would also help Chantal financially. We thought about a honeymoon, and it so happened that Dora Basilio and her new husband Paolo Rodriguez Lima had invited us to Rio, and at Easter of the next year we flew from Paris to meet them at Rio de Janeiro airport

Paolo was a retired civil engineer, we had already met him in London at the flat when we also invited Douglas Cochrane, an old friend also of Dora, and a school friend of mine.

They had a flat not far from Ipanema beach, guarded I was surpised to see by railings and a watchman sitting outside. They had a live-in maid, Maria, and introduced us to Paolo's family, and had planned visits to places in Rio, and a weekend in Petropolis in the hills nearby.

Cutting the cake

We were taken to many interesting places by Dora and Paolo, and Dora introduced me to some important people in the art world with the possible idea of having a show there, but nothing much came of it. We saw the Museum of Modern Art which seemed something of a white elephant, and the Museum designed by Niemeyer, like a flying saucer hovering by the sea, however inside it did not seem to me to be so impressive. The Botanical Gardens were superb and they had a nursery where plants could be bought by the public. I bought two Ravenala madagascariensis, the travellers tree, which I cossetted as far as my garden in Gozo, but they did not survive. The garden had long dark avenues of exotic trees, and a little café where we had lunch, also a rather neglected Japanese garden.

Chantal, Paolo and Dora at the Niemeyer Contemporary Art Museum, Rio

We also made the pilgimage to the statue of Christ at Corcovado in a funicular, reminding me of the much much smaller one in Gozo! We visited two painters in their houses in the country from Petropolis, with splendid gardens on the edge of the jungle. I had hoped to see a sloth, but although I was told they were around, did not have the luck to see one.

Dora and Paolo had a small apartment in a central block in Petropolis, and we stayed a few nights. One evening I cooked spaghetti, and another we ate at a restaurant where you took your plate with food to be weighed, and you paid accordingly.

Back in Rio we sat on the beach at Ipanema and watched the attractive Brazilian girls parade on the sand, and saw the house of the author of 'The Girl from Ipanema.' Nearby we saw the police arrest a man with a gun, and Paolo admonished us for venturing off the main streets of their neighbourhood. On our last evening I invited them to a big Italian restaurant at Copacabana, on the sea-front. It was April, but pleasantly warm.

We had been shepherded around by Paolo and Dora, with the best intentions, but we wanted to escape for a week on our own, and instead of going to Minas Gerais where they had planned for us, we took a plane to Florianopolis, a big island in the south of Brazil. It was connected by a bridge to the mainland, and we stayed a night in the town, and then took a bus to Santo Antonio, a small fishing village on the west side of the island. The bus stopped on the outskirts of the village, near a restaurant, and we left our luggage there as we walked down to the sea. There was not much accommodation in the small village, but a German woman had a complex of bungalows in an attractive garden, and we stayed there for two or three nights.

Santo Antonio was charming, there was a small outdoor restaurant at the sea and they made some excellent pasta and fish. We relaxed sitting on the beach, admiring the strange rocks that emerged from the water, reminding me of the Brittany coast.

We hired a local taxi to take us further around the island, which had a huge lagoon in the centre and a wonderful restaurant whose fare consisted almost entirely of prawns: first, second and third courses. The taxi driver took us on to Jurere where again we had good food, and met a French family.

The painter we had met near Petropolis was John Nicholson, and he was doing large geometrical paintings with which I felt I had something in common. He was American by birth, but had been living a long time in Brazil, and he visited us in Paris after having a show in Switzerland.

I mentioned earlier my friendship with Ivan Alechine, and for a couple of weeks I swapped the house in Gozo for his place in rue Brezin, in the 14th *arrondissement* in Paris.

Ivan often came to Gozo, and visited us with his new wife Mercedes at rue d'Anjou. He is a poet and spent much time in Mexico.

As I mentioned earlier Chantal and I decided to spend our Christmases in different places, one year in Barcelona which we loved, then in Dubrovnik, Vienna, Berlin, and Rome. Generally we were back in time for the New Year and saw Franck and his family with a Christmas tree and crackers.

Rather as in Italy Christmas was not celebrated in France quite in the same way as in England with the rituals of presents, turkey and plum pudding. However the French children seemed to like Christmas crackers if not the pudding.

Ivan Alechine and myself at the Grand Palais

In Berlin we visited Kathleen Michael, the dancer, and her boyfriend, living in the Gneisenau Strasse, reminding me of the war and the battleships Scharnhorst and Gneisenau! Berlin was fascinating and we went to the principal museums, seeing the head of Nefertiti, and the wonderful Watteau painting, 'The Enseigne de Gersaint' at the Charlottenberg palace.

Also the great collection of Berggruen with its Picassos and Klees.

We had a strange day at an extraordinary place south of Berlin by train. It is called 'Tropical Islands' and is a hangar providing the second largest free-standing volume in the world: it was originally a hangar for zeppelins and was now a resort with beaches, rain-forest, restaurants, hills and even theatres.

It was less than an hour by train on a miserably cold day, and we took a shuttle from the railway siding to the hangar. Inside the temperature was kept at 26° and many of the several hundred visitors were in bathing suits. The time of day was imitated with the lighting, and it was possible to stay the night. We ate at a good Thai restaurant and saw a show of dancing. We walked in the forest and sat for a while on deckchairs near the 'sea'. Sceptics thought it could not pay for itself, but it seems to be still thriving. It reminds me a little of the film 'The Truman Show': a self-contained world with its own sea.

Brian Catling, his son Jack, and Chantal in Oxford

We were now going to London only about once a year as we no longer had the Kings Road flat to stay in. We stayed rather at the Chelsea Arts Club or once or twice at bed-sitters in Chelsea. We would see Brian and Sarah in Oxford as well as the Burke-Borrowes, and my cousin Peter at Harrow. In recent years we have rented a self-catering flat at Nell Gwynn House in Sloane Avenue for a week, usually at the beginning of March, when I also see the cardiologist at London Bridge Hospital. Do I miss London? Rather as Florence I miss friends, but I do not believe I would ever want to live there again, in spite of which I still read the Daily Telegraph every day and keep more in touch with British news than French or Italian; or Maltese for that matter.

We also went down to Horsham to see my old school friend Oliver Evans Palmer (photo on page 11) in Horsham: He had more or less retired from his job in Building Standards but still attended conferences and debates.

We went down to Brighton and I showed Chantal where I used to live, and found my old studio, in a still run-down courtyard. We had lunch at English's, excellent fish and sea food, and walked along the beach. Chantal has a great affinity with the sea. Unfortunately the last time we were there the little railway that runs along the sea front to Black Rock was not open until Easter. Back in Paris we spent a New Year's Eve at '*Le Cléopâtre*' and sometimes went to other *clubs libertins* . Research for my paintings? Part of Parisian life.

Speaking of erotica I sometimes contributed to Jamie Maclean's 'Erotic

Review', edited at the time by Rowan Pelling. I fell out to some degree with Jamie. He proposed a book on my work, but as a result of a computerised poll it was never published; he had then proposed a new edition of 'Sophie's Dream Book' for which I worked on a number of alterations at his suggestion, but that also never saw the light of day.

On one of our visits to London I decided to hire a car and drive down to Devon with Chantal, and show her where my grandparents had lived. We stopped on the way at Lyme Regis in Dorset, then on to Torquay where I had hoped to see the little courtyard where my grandfather's studio had been, afterwards taken over by Breon O'Casey, Sean O'Casey's son. Alas, it had been demolished and a terrace of pseudo Georgian houses built in its place.

The same thing happened when we went to Newton Ferrers to see 'Waydown', which I knew had been renamed 'The Studio'. There were wooden steps up to the entrance, and at the top a building site, no Waydown. There was a surveyor at work: two villas were to be built there.

I spoke to a woman who lived opposite, and she said it had become difficult for the locals to continue living in the village: prices had shot up, and these two villas were going to cost several hundred thousand pounds.

We went on to Plymouth and stayed a night near the Hoe, and I went the next day to the Art Museum and spoke to one of the curators about my grandfather. They knew of him of course, but did not seem overly enthusiastic about his work.

Back to London via a night at Salisbury where we visited the cathedral and saw their copy of the Magna Carta. On the whole this was a disappointing trip, and I did not want to pass by Radnor as I knew I would be saddened by the changes that had also taken place there, even though I would have liked Chantal to see the place of my childhood and early life.

Myself with pages from my book

Back in France we made several visits to Brittany, one for a baptism of the son of Christian, Chantal's brother. It was a big family meeting and dinner, and we saw the new house with a splendid interior, that Christian had built. We also visited another brother, Alain, who had a very attractive old stone house. His wife sadly suffered from MS, and died a few years later, but his daughters, Virginie and Anaick, later came with Jean-Claude's daughter Amélie to visit us in Gozo for a holiday. I also painted a wedding portrait of another brother,

Serge, and his wife Veronique, with a background of the sea. Not the first time that I had painted a portrait as a wedding present!

One summer in Gozo we took a short cruise in a renamed French liner to Naples and Messina, two nights on board. The crew was a great mix of nationalities, the food was good and there was a cabaret in the evenings, and even a small gaming room. We dropped anchor in the port of Naples, and were taken by bus first to Sorrento, where I saw in the distance the villa of Friedl Schorr's friends, the Schelers: if indeed it still belonged to them, and then to Pompeii where I had been before, but Chantal had not. We saw the erotic murals and were taken around by a guide. In spite of the tourism the place still had an extraordinary atmosphere where you could imagine the life as it was in the days of Pliny the Younger.

The next day we went to Messina, and after a bus tour via Catania to Etna to see the embers of the volcano, and the lava, we returned to Taormina where we saw the arena and bought a big fruit dish for Gozo.

Chantal in Taormina

We made another trip to Florence, this time staying in a convent in Borgo Pinti, of the order Oblate dell' Assunzione, originally a French order and most of the *suore* spoke French. We went to see Vittoria and Andrea who had now moved their studio from its previous address in Via Anguillara to Via Bentacordi, not far away. It was a big job displacing their great etching press. We went with them to see Susan Loewenherz and her husband Paolo at Torano, Carrara, lunching in their favourite restaurant near the quarries

Paolo showed us the lifesize copy of a Cadillac in marble which he had been working on for some time, so realistic that you felt the wheels would turn and the car would take off!

With Ilaria we passed by my old apartment in Via de Bardi and spoke to the concierge who told us that the flat had been sold by the Capponis to a leather manufacturer for a vast sum. John Pope Hennessy had died, and there was a plaque on the wall of the palazzo in his honour. I wondered if there would ever be one in mine. I

Vittoria and Andrea in their studio in Florence

very much doubted it. I was not especially friendly with the Capponis, and what is a mere painter compared to a famous art historian?!

In Paris the flat in rue d'Anjou was becoming expensive. There are two taxes on property in France, the *Taxe foncière*, and the *Taxe d'habitation*. As both of us were now resident in Malta, the tax was increased. In 2005 we started looking for somewhere less expensive and perhaps less pretentious to live, and had a look at various other quartiers in Paris. We also liked places like Saint Germain en Laye, but these opulent suburbs were nearly as expensive.

One town we had visited and liked was Compiègne: it was only 45 minutes by train from the Gare du Nord, and an attractive town in the middle of a forest, with its great Château, opera house, and park and gardens. The centre was medieval, with its churches of Saint Jacques and Saint Antoine: the latter having been visited at Mass five times by Jeanne d'Arc.

We saw a possible place to buy, an ex créperie, but first we had to sell the flat in rue d'Anjou, which was not going to be easy.

I was still working in the studio in rue Oberkampf, and having moulds made by Monsieur Gasc of the terracottas I had fired by my neighbour. The artisans in the small *cour* had an open studio weekend, and I had sculptures and paintings on show. I have to say I was not selling much, apart from erotic drawings to an important Paris collector, and the odd book.

Chantal and Susan with marble Cadillac

Chantal visited various agents about selling the Paris flat. An English agency specialising in châteaux and important Paris properties, and other smaller agencies. One problem was that they all wanted exclusivity. We did not dare, of course, finalise a purchase in Compiègne until we had sold the flat. Finally, a relatively small agency not far from us in Paris proposed a client, a Tanzanian originally from Zanzibar, who was a financier educated in London, and who was looking for a place to entertain: his sister was married to a diplomat working nearby, and by now we had emptied the place and its grand volumes could be seen at an advantage.

He bought the flat at the price we asked, and although the Créperie in Compiègne fell through due to a less than honest vendor, we bought another, more central property, on three floors, with a huge garage and shop that was let and produced a good income, on the ground floor.

We were lucky to be able to buy this place, but once again Chantal was quick off the mark, we saw it and decided as soon as it was in the hands of an agency in Compiègne. The great advantage for me would be the space to make a studio, and store my paintings. Then we would have two floors living space, an attic, a library and office for me. We were thankful in the end not to have bought the Crêperie which had less space and was farther away from the centre of town, and the railway station. Now came the traumatic process of moving house.

51 rue de Paris, Compiègne

14

COMPIEGNE

Messrs Oudinot carried out the removals to Compiègne, as they had done several years ago from rue Beaubourg. Fortunately their van was able to park in the street outside and everything could be loaded down by a lift. It was, as usual, a big operation, and it took me some days to pack and label the dozens of cardboard cartons for papers and small objects, not to mention the books which would have to keep their shelf numbers for my new library in Compiègne.

We had been fortunate in finding a Sri Lankan jack-of-all-trades called Rajah who reassembled my bookshelves around the four walls of the library. They had travelled from Radnor, to Florence, to rue Beaubourg, to rue d'Anjou, and now here. The round table which we had used as a dining table in rue Beaubourg was now in the centre of the library, already overloaded with books. The now rather tatty Aubusson carpet fitted the library as well.

A colleague of Chantal's brother Franck, from Brittany, but now living in Paris, David, undertook to make a studio for me out of the back part of the garage. With the help of his father-in-law this was separated by a breeze-block wall with a door, and tiled. Also another skylight had to be made, and the studio was ready. It was a marvellous space, but soon to be cluttered again with all the boxes and wrapping material, as well as my paintings and sculptures. To this day it has not all been sorted out!

Adjoining the studio, as well as the library, I made an office about the same size as the one I had had in rue d'Anjou, and here I had my computer and a bookcase with reference works: my Littré dictionary, Encyclopedia Britannica, Arthur Mee's extraordinary pictorial encyclopedia 'I See All', many other dictionaries and computer manuals. Above the computer one of my favourite British paintings in the form of a mezzotint: Sir Noel Paton's 'The Quarrel of Oberon and Titania.'

Above the shop there were two flats, on the first and second floors. We had to do considerable reconstruction to turn this into a maisonette with living-room, dining-room and kitchen on the first floor, and three bedrooms and bathroom as well as a walk-in closet on the second floor.

This work entailed removing walls, making a bathroom and kitchen, and a *buanderie* for the washing machine. This all took time, but was ready by the time we had given up the Paris flat.

Outside the living room was a roof where evidently there had been a terrace, and we opened this up and bought plants and trellis to make it a pleasant place to eat outside in the warmer weather. Here I could grow a few rhododendrons in pots which I was unable to do in Gozo due to the limey soil.

Roof terrace in Compiègne

It took a while to settle in, and Compiègne was not Paris. However it had great charm and our house was very convenient for shopping, and near to the station for Paris, as I believe I have said before. We bought a large television with a Sky box for English programmes, and Chantal had the French television in the spare room upstairs. We did not have a car, leaving the old car in Gozo to be looked after by Gigi Dimech when not there.

My library, Compiègne

I now had about 3000 books in my new library, finally all in the same room. I found an extraordinary site on the internet, librarything.com, and managed to catalogue all the books, and indicate which shelf they were on.

I was getting more and more seduced by the computer and what it can do, and produced a catalogue of most of my geometrical paintings of the nineteen sixties, using the print-on-demand site lulu.com.

Before leaving rue d'Anjou I had been searching for a yellow file which contained all the poetry I had written while in Florence, and before. While rearranging my books in my new library, I finally found it. There were more than fifty poems and I decided to make another book of them to publish on

164

lulu.com under the title of 'David Russell, Poems from the Fifties'. I was very happy with the result: after not having read the poems for about thirty years I was surprised at their quality, if I say so myself!

I was now spending a lot of time at the computer, making a photo archive of my paintings, learning to use Photoshop. I had done a course in Paris of Word and Photoshop in a small school near St Lazare with a teacher who spoke good English. I am not sure if the general public has realised how far these IT programmes have changed the appearance of magazines and newspapers, but as with the digital camera the change has been enormous, even if one could say that the quality of design has not kept pace with the technical advantages.

I also bought an iPod and downloaded much of my favourite music. Mozart, Monteverdi, the madrigals we had sung in Florence, Scarlatti, Roberto Murolo's Neapolitan songs. I have not yet mentioned my love of Rossini. When living in Italy I tried to see any Rossini opera that was going, though I never got to Pesaro. With Ilaria I went to Venice where we saw 'L'Italiana in Algeri' which I think is my favourite of his operas. Also in Venice I saw 'Tancredi' with Marilyn Horne, the mezzo-soprano. I sometimes think of Rossini in tandem with Duchamp: both virtuosi giving up the practice of their great talents at one stage in their lives.

On librarything.com there is a facility for contacting like-minded book lovers, and in 2006 I started a conversation with a mysterious American woman under the name of Sandrine, which has been going until today.

Although I have a great library I do not use it enough. I am too addicted to crime novels and the television. I am also ashamed to say that I do not use my magnificent studio to paint enough. I had my mother's and grandfather's paintings and effects stored at Rogers in London, and had them brought to Compiègne by a man from Hamburg, and sorting and storing them has been something of a nightmare. At the time of writing this there is still a lot of clearing up to do, exhibitions to arrange, and the paintings stored near Cologne to be brought home.

The Mairie Compiègne at night

2007 saw my eightieth birthday, and we decided to have a party in Florence. Joss and Antonio helped greatly with this arrangement. We invited about twenty old friends to lunch on the rooftop restaurant of the Pitti Palace Hotel, near the Ponte Vecchio.

Ilaria and Vittoria and Andrea were not able to come, but Donald and Caroline brought me a magnificent bunch of 80 gerberas, and Susan Arcamone came with her two sons, and Joss and Antonio brought a birthday cake.

We stayed at the Annalena pensione where I had stayed many years before. It had a long history from the time of the Medicis, and most of the rooms had a terrace. Susan took us up to Fiesole where we had tea at the Bencista, and dinner with Joss and Antonio on their terrace at Isolotto.

Susan also took us to Harold Acton's villa La Pietra where I had never before been. It was now part of New York University and had strict rules about visitors. I remembered Acton at the Villa Ombrellino, and how Violet Trefusis often entertained him, and how insulting he was about her after her death.

The villa was beautifully maintained, especially the gardens which the university had lately brought up to scratch.

Chantal at La Pietra

We also visited Lapo Binazzi and Ilaria Galli, and had dinner with the mystery writer Magdalen Nabb in Via Romana, whom we heard most sadly a few weeks later had died of a heart attack.

For the last twenty or so years I had been buying my nylon socks in Florence at a *merceria* called Quercioli e Lucchesini. I usually bought eight or ten pairs at a time, however they moved their premises to give way to an important franchise store, and now I have to look on the internet to find my socks: no other shop appears to stock them!

Like most people I suppose, it came as a shock to me to realise I had passed the eighty-year-old mark. My health was not bad, although I was on the edge of diabetes and had to restrain my love of sugar. Although I had had one cataract operated on in my right eye, I had another to come but which the opthalmologist said I could put off for the time being. My chief disability was my hearing which was steadily getting worse. To watch television I took to using earphones with a wireless connection, but my chief problem was in restaurants. Even with sophisticated hearing aids the background noise was often too much. I thought of the Aged P in Great Expectations, or of Goldoni's Signor Todero who thinks his little handbell is broken because he cannot hear it ring. No, it was not as bad as that, but music suffered except for the iPod which came across loud and clear.

Memory was also beginning to lapse, and in this respect Google was of great help, for example in writing these memoirs in the years where I no longer had a diary to rely on. For information purposes what a saving of time Google provides instead of going to the library for research.

I am really happy to have lived to see such technological marvels, and can only imagine what the future will bring in, say, twenty years time from now, global warming permitting.

In Gozo I now also had a PC and was able to work there as well on my books. In 2008 my neighbour, an American psychiatrist who hardly ever came to Gozo complained about tree-roots from my garden penetrating under our dividing rubble wall into her small empty garden. She has now brought an action against me in Gozo tribunal, and I wait to see the outcome. Trees planted more than thirty years before are supposed to be exempt from being chopped down: we will see!

Myself and Chantal at Florence birthday party

A sad event occurred in the summer of 2009. A very old friend, Jan Pettigrew, who had a house in Gharb, Gozo, died in Thailand. Her husband James had died many years before, and Jan was living on her own, looked after by local women, as her memory was beginning to fade and she was no longer strong physically. She had a stepson who was resident in Thailand and married to a local girl, and he persuaded Jan to move to his house. She agreed to go for a holiday, but was quite soon put in a nursing home near Bangkok where she died. As she had always asked to be buried near her husband in Gozo I asked the stepson to send her ashes back, but got a frosty reply.

Jan was a fashion illustrator under her maiden name, Jan Langan, and I saw a lot of Jan and James in London, having a house in Belgravia before moving to Gozo. She was sophisticated and amusing, and Chantal and I both adored her. She was a great loss to the small group of expatriates living on the island.

Being resident in Gozo however was not an unalloyed blessing as we had tax complications, Chantal also being considered resident there which affected taxes in France. We are still trying to overcome these bureaucratic hurdles. But I work well there, and painted a series of canvases in these recent years illustrated in the following pages, making use once again of the Camera Lucida bought so many years ago in Paris, albeit works on a small scale. I read with interest David Hockney's book on the subject of the Camera Lucida snd tend to agree with a lot of his conclusions, in respect of Vermeer for example. There is a treatment of light obtained through using the device that cannot be had in any other way and that has different properties from photography, or copies of photography in paint.

The garden in Gozo is maturing with the help of Leli Farrugia who looks after it twice a week, and Liza and Joe Mintoff who have looked after the house for the last thirty years. I cannot now do the heavier work that I used to, and as the garden is now full of trees, shrubs and plants, I have somewhat lost interest in growing rarities from seed, or trying to find unusual plants that would suit the Maltese climate.

As it is, there are three or four places to eat outside in the garden which is a great joy, and there are new supermarkets in Victoria where I do my shopping most mornings. The lampuki, or dolphin fish, arrives in August-September, and is a great local delicacy. There is a good variety of fish, also now a frozen goods store which has products from France, Italy and Germany. Gozo is becoming modernised, but without losing most of its traditions, for example the village festas with their church processions, statues of saints and firework displays.

I would hope never to have to give up this house. It does not have perhaps as many memories as the Radnor of my youth, but nevertheless I have passed many happy days and months there. I am lucky also to have my studio and library in Compiègne, where I hope to work for some time to come, near my dear wife Chantal.

Maenad 2007

Chariot with smoke 2003

Two women talking   terracotta

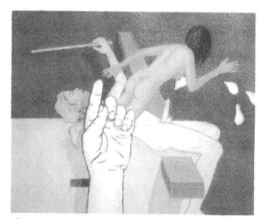
Pointing hand 2004

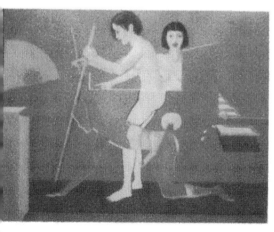
Girls back-to-back terracotta

Women with sticks 2004

Recent paintings and sculptures

Abstract Love 2004

Girls in orange room 2006

Girl with baton 2005

At the breast terracotta

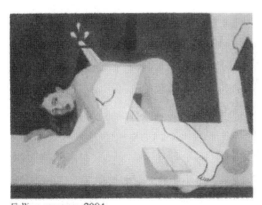
Falling woman 2004

Wedge 2002

Recent paintings and sculptures

15

ENVOI

Although I now rarely visit England and London, I keep in touch with what is going on there through the papers and television. The art scene looks appalling, highly commercialised and superficial. Damian Hirst, considered one of the most important English painters, painted a series of canvasses with dots. This had been done much better in the sixties in a comic book 'Little Dot in Dotland.' The misunderstanding of Duchamp's intellectual propositions has been responsible for any amount of valueless and boring work by young artists, together with the pretentious 'political correctness' imported from the US which dumbs down art in the name of 'creativity' for all.

Little Dot in Dotland

In a way I hesitate to express these opinions, as I may easily be accused of fogeyism or not understanding the young generation of artists. On the other hand I welcome unconditionally the technical advances which have led to computer generated films, for example, though it is a pity that few artists of the stature of Fischinger at the Bauhaus appear to be using the medium. The appearance of magazines and publicity has changed enormously in my lifetime due to printing processes, and I may add Photoshop, sometimes to the good: art magazines and books have benefited greatly in colour reproduction. I hope to produce these memoirs by publishing them on lulu.com, an extraordinary print-on-demand company in the United States.

Travel has become much easier; going to London from Paris as I do once or twice a year is comfortable and quick on the Eurostar as compared with the Golden Arrow of years past. Communication via the internet is now virtually instantaneous, bringing about the possibility proposed by Joseph Beuys of a country ruled democratically by referendum. Perhaps this will come about one day though public opinion in England looks like being less and less well informed and more and more concentrated on football and 'celebrities'.

Then there is the sexual revolution. Having worked with erotica this interests me a lot. The subjective difference between erotic and pornographic. Nigel Kneale's television play from the sixties 'The Year of the Sex Olympics' foreshadows the porn industry from California. Today 'having sex' is little different from 'having breakfast'. As has often been pointed out, the mystery and excitement of the erotic goes by the board in a purely athletic attitude to sexuality. It is the human and cerebral interaction that is interesting, combined with the desire or attraction. Place, dress, ambience all have their importance. Sometimes in American porn movies there is a 'modern' painting on the wall behind the actors, but this is more to show us that this is a classy place than contributing to the erotic atmosphere. The atmosphere is minimal, the bodies everything. At least this is not hypocritical: before there had to be a totally false story of seduction. Here it is the women's bodies that are important, the men's much less so, and the men's faces and expressions not at all. The genitals devoid of the veil of pubic hair, and the breasts are the key players in the drama, if it can be so called. It is certainly a new form of cinema with its own rules, and state of the art technique in lighting and photography.

I love the cinema, but have difficulty with understanding French films, which I never had with Italian speaking ones. After more than ten years I am still not really attuned to French: I have an idea that it is the form of thought more than the language, the supposed logic and clarity often escape me!

In 2008 as I have mentioned before, I published a book of poems entitled 'Poems from the Fifties.' I was very happy the way this turned out, with its cover taken from my mural in Gozo, and the memories of what now seem innocent times. One of the things I most regret not having done in my life is writing more, and another is acting. But I am never happier than when painting.

Old age creeps up suddenly, and of course carries with it many restrictions. But I fancy it is easier for those who lived through the war years to accept unfavourable conditions. I am lucky to have my work, a big studio, and a loving wife.

Poems from the fiftties

Although I keep up with news from the UK I cannot imagine, at this stage in my life, going back to live there. I am at home in Gozo and love the Mediterranean, and here in France Paris is near enough to provide an intellectual stimulus. I dream a lot, possibly due to the various pills I take for my heart problems, and most of these dreams are either of Radnor or Italy.

In October 2009 I stopped off in Florence on my way back to France for five days. I stayed at the convent of the Oblate dell'Assunzione in Borgo Pinti. I saw my old friends, Antonio and Joss, Vittoria and Andrea, Lapo Binazzi, and of course Ilaria.

Myself at Ilaria's flat in Florence

On the last evening I had dinner with Joss, Antonio, Don and Caroline at 'Il Sabatino', a trattoria I had never been to before, near the Porta san Frediano.

It was like the old days in Florence when we used to eat nearly every day at 'Le Sorelle'. A simple place, good food, and good company.

Some *scorci* from my memories: Sir Francis, my godfather, looking like Michael Caine with fly-swatter in hand, reciting word for word Dan Leno's sketch ' The Tower of London'; my mother tap-dancing and trying to teach me the steps; Margaret diving off the point in Gozo with Mick Gelbhauer; Ingrid at the railway station in Konstanz; Chantal eating prawns on the beach in Phuket; the early morning at Radnor in the snow with deer eating the rose bushes.

Now back to my easel!

Printed in Great Britain
by Amazon